Wokin
Glo

STAINED GLASS

Stained Glass

Poetry from the Land of Mozambique

Edited by Luis Rafael

ROMAN *Books*
www.roman-books.co.uk

Editorial Copyright © 2011 Luis Rafael

Low-price Edition ISBN 978-93-80905-08-2

Typeset in Palatino Linotype

First Published 2011
Low-price Edition 2012

1 3 5 7 9 8 6 4 2

British Library Cataloguing in Publication Data
A catalogue record for this book is available from the British Library

ROMAN Books
26 York Street, London W1U 6PZ, United Kingdom
2nd Floor, 38/3, Andul Road, Howrah 711109, WB, India
www.roman-books.co.uk | www.roman-books.co.in

Printed and bound in India by
Roman Printers Private Limited
www.romanprinters.com

In memoriam
M. V. F.

CONTENTS

The Poetry of Mozambique

'I come from a dream country'
Ana Mafalda Leite

In the Land of Sheik Moosa Ibn Biq'

Mozambique is a thin stretch of country next to the Indian Ocean. Such a
long coastline tells a story of multiple navigations, multiple visitations. An
African country, its name is Arabic, and the Portuguese who colonized its
coastal regions for a long time governed it as a far-off outpost of Goa, in
India. Many of the country's original inhabitants had arrived there from
different parts of Africa, driven by the internal migrations within the
continent, but the land was also visited by many other people, not only the
Arabs and the Portuguese, but also Turks, Indonesians, Indians, the
Chinese. These different visitors left their traces on the land. Sometimes
these traces were submerged under the new tongues, the new stories, of
subsequent visitors:

> Because in the beginning there was the sea and the Island. Sinbad and Ulysses.
> Scheherazade and Penelope. Names over names. Tongue from tongues, multiple
> matricide in Makua.

The Arabs gave the coastal people their religion: and in Mozambique
today there are more Muslims than there are Christians. The Portuguese
gave them a language of 'national unity'. The poetry in this anthology was
all written in Portuguese.

Race and the Politics of Language

The poetry of Mozambique is rooted, first of all, in the light, the sea, and
the people of that country. Because it is rooted in these things it is very
difficult to work out what the colour is of the skin behind the text. The
poets of Mozambique have been black, Indian, Goan, mulatto, white. The

presence of all these ethnic communities resulted in multiple convergences, sometimes epidermal, but also textual:

> [we are] together in the spiral of a
> black and white
> raceless
> dream!

No one will deny that epidermal configurations do exist behind the words of the poem, but these are better gleaned, not from the poem, but from biographies. And biographies are not poems.

Or, to rephrase: in terms of my criteria for selection I have not used biographies as poems. God knows, there are enough people who elevate biographies to the status of poems, only so that they can be excluded from the ultimate canon. I have often heard it said, especially within the red-brick walls of some South African universities, that blacks cannot really write poetry. Conversely, many black South Africans have told me, in conversation, that whites and Indians can never be African poets, which is quite true, if one is going to call them 'whites' and 'Indians'. Not so far back, in South Africa, a (black) Mozambican poet was howled at for speaking in Portuguese (a white language). I, who had translated what he had said, was attacked because, as I was told, I should have been translating from the Swahili, a black language. But as I pointed out at the time, even Swahili is not that 'black'; it owes much to the Arabic, as does Portuguese. There is no pure language.

If these problems are real enough to South Africans, they are less real to Mozambicans. Whereas a South African like Lesego Rampolokeng can still express angst and anger about being forced to write in the English language—

> I only fight the British
> with the bullets that are English[1]

—the Mozambicans treat the Portuguese language as one of their spoils of war. Exactly said: "The Portuguese language is a war trophy."[2] These words were spoken by the Angolan, José Luandino Vieira, but they could just as easily have been said by a Mozambican. It is because Mozambicans are confident that the language belongs to them that they can make it more Mozambican. Often, in Mozambican poetry, Portuguese converges with African languages: it takes on their vocabulary, morphology, syntax, and in

14

the process, as the language become richer, more plastic, it suggests fresh horizons, new ways of saying new things.

Our Village Is a Very Big Place

A country of many cultures, but also a country of many poets, Mozambique is not really a country of prose writers. There have of course been brilliant excursions into prose: there was Luis Bernardo Honwana in the 1960s with his *Who Killed Mangy-Dog?*, and in the 1980s there was Ungulani ba ka Khosa who writes with classical severity, and there was Mia Couto whose playful handling of language creates a diction shot with original splendour. But, then again, Mia Couto started off as a poet.

The fact that Mozambique has produced so many poets is surprising, given that until recently the country had a 90% rate of illiteracy. There are many reasons why people turn to poetry. Poetry, for one, is cheaper to publish than prose: in Mozambique, where newspapers do print poetry, there is always a greater readiness to publish a short poem rather than a larger prose work. Then there is the question of censorship. This is more true of the colonial period, although we could perhaps subsume the idea of political or ideological correctness (surely a variant of self-censorship?) under the rubric, which would make the idea of censorship as pertinent to the period after independence as it was to the period that came before. Books, stories, pamphlets are always too suspect; the poem with its compressed hermetic form, its subtle use of language, its often impenetrable allusions, allowed escape from easy detection. A neat political weapon. But then again, if the poet wanted to wanted to cry out loudly enough, if that poet was determined to speak about the things that were happening, the poem remained an appropriate medium of communication: the poem, usually small, typed on a single sheet, could be carried around, it could be read at meetings or in the silence of the night, away from the omniscient eyes of the censor.

The Intimate Logic of the Poem

But enough on how certain types of poetry get to be written. Mozambican poetry has a greatness, which is also political, but which has nothing to do with the necessary politics of sabotage, the fugitive texts of midnight protest poetry. My favourite explanation of what constitutes the committed poetic text comes from Sophia Andresen, one of Portugal's finest poets, and a significant, if sometimes hidden, influence on the world of Mozambican poetry. Sophia writes:

> Whoever searches for a just relation with the stone, the tree, the river, is inevitably taken, by the spirit of truth which enlivens him, to search for a just relation with the human being. The one that sees the frightful splendour of the world is logically taken to see the frightful suffering of the world. It is merely a question of attention, sequence, rigour . . . If when we are faced by the splendour of the world we rejoice with passion, when we are faced by the suffering of the world we are outraged with equal passion. This logic is intimate, inwards, a consequence of its own self, necessary, faithful to itself.[3]

The greatest Mozambican poetry is faithful to this 'intimate logic' of the poem. Much of Mozambican poetry is a song of praise to the elements and, in particular, it sings the sea, which is the most primal of all truths: the tides, life, the horizon end:

> Why is it always the sea:
> It's that
> —the dead, the seaweed, the tides, the living.

By the same logic, this poetry is a testimony of the human will and its suffering under the successive tyrannies of history; it is an encounter with the ghosts of slavery, forced labour, war and its massacres, armed banditry and its horrors. The sheer intensity of this nightmare often resists easy words with which to describe it. It might call for a violent disruption of literary form, syntax, words, as we witness in Luís Carlos Patraquim's monument to the horror, "Carnivorous Elegy", the closest Mozambican poetry can approximate the vision of Malangatana's panels with their crazy, twisted and lurid faces shining out of a night of darkness:

> . . . the haemorrhage of fear
> in the eyes of the cane, the memory of the land
> sucking itself in the avenged aortas

But sometimes there are no words, there is no response adequate to the immensity of the crime. There is silence. And at times the silence merges with the white light of day, the wake on the water, the unending horizon of sea. The maritime motifs are transmuted, through a process of emplacement, into visual indices of the silence:

16

> ... all words,
> all calls, shouts, tears
> are dispersed into the shadow of the wind
> and into the secret blue of the water.

And here is the greatness of Mozambican poetry. The poetry of Mozambique and, in particular, that of its greatest interpreters, people like José Craveirinha, Glória de Sant'Anna, Luís Carlos Patraquim, sings of the immensity and wonder of the Indian Ocean and also the anguish of a people who many times in their past have been forced to inhabit a nightmare. It reserves the rage for the inhumanity and the praise for all the splendid things of the earth. It is a poetry born out of logic and lucidity—a lesson that was learnt from the water.

Johannesburg, November 1993

Some Brief Notes on the Criteria for the Selection of Authors

This is a selection of poems from Mozambique. Most of the poems were written in Mozambique and most were also published there. The poets included were, however, not necessarily born in Mozambique. If I have not used place of birth as a criterion for selection, neither have I paid much attention to whether or not the poet spent most of his/her life inside Mozambique. Exile has been a permanent feature of the Mozambican literary scene, both before and after independence.

I have accepted as Mozambican any work that was written or published in Mozambique or which, if it was written and published elsewhere, was about Mozambique, even if this Mozambique was an imagined one. Imaginary worlds are imaginary only up to a point; they usually arise out of some historical reality.

But there are limits to representativeness. I have not assigned the same weight to each of the selected poets. Some poets are better represented than others. These are usually the older poets, who have published more.

Some readers—schooled in earlier anthologies of protest poetry, especially Margaret Dickison's *When Bullets Begin to Flower* (1972) and Chris Searle's *The Sunflower of Hope* (1982) —might find that some of the names they thought of as being representative of Mozambican poetry have been excluded from this selection. But that is the problem with thematic anthologies: Mozambican poetry was never just (that type of) protest poetry. It is true that it was, and we have the evidence of José Craveirinha and Noémia de Sousa's fine poems of hope and outrage. But what of the discreet voice of someone like Glória de Sant'Anna whose protest poems on the colonial war (1964-1974) were published only in 1988? Do we ignore her poetry, as most anthologisers have done, simply because we did not search hard enough to find her poems or because her name wasn't on the post-revolutionary lips of some Mozambican intellectuals. There are many ways to write protest poetry.

There are also many ways to write poetry. Mozambique has a wealth of poetic traditions. We should not ignore these other traditions simply because they do not fit in with our prior conceptions. And while I have tried not to ignore the historically important protest poetry, it is the range of voices, the variety of traditions, that I have tried to present. No selection can be entirely fair. A selection arrives, pre-packaged, with all types of biases and presuppositions. I hope to have been honest about some of mine.

More Notes, Added Ten Years Later . . .

This anthology was ready for publication when I left South Africa in August 1994. The anthology had originally been conceived for a South African public, and in many ways this made sense: the world closest to Mozambique is the one with which it shares a border: South Africa. So much of Mozambican poetry returns, obsessively, to the 'problem' of South Africa. It is easy to understand why. For a long time the Mozambican economy was kept afloat through the money South Africa paid to use Mozambican migrant workers to work on the Rand mines. In the days of apartheid, white South Africans used to holiday in Mozambique and they used to walk the town barefoot, throwing banana peels wherever they went, and at night, away from home, many used to savour sweet night-secrets with black prostitutes; either way, they offered Mozambicans an inside view into their arrogance and their hypocritical *baasskap*. More insidiously, in the 1980s South Africans, from their bases in the Eastern Transvaal and their offices in Pretoria, engineered a policy of 'destabilisation' that would earn them over a million corpses. But these were not the only South Africans that Mozambicans knew, for there were exiles from apartheid tyranny living and working in Mozambique, and many of these are heroes to Mozambicans: Ruth First, for example, who was working at the university when she was killed by a parcel bomb. All these things, and more, contribute to an image of South Africa. It is a refracted image, to be sure, perhaps because it is observed from a the perspective of an altogether different culture, or perhaps because from this vantage point different details are seen. Although Mozambican poetry does not function solely as an inverted mirror of South Africa, I always thought that this point of connection would have intrigued educated South Africans, would have made them want to know more. When I started sending translations to literary journals in South Africa there was a genuine interest in the literary production of Mozambique; but this was before I left the country. The publishers I approached after I had left the country fobbed me off with excuses like: "This is all very interesting, but no one will read it." Or: "We can't be sure that you know Portuguese well enough to translate Mozambican poetry." Even promises of funding, available at the time, were not sufficient to entice anyone. Either Mozambican poetry was really too dreadful or maybe my politics (whatever they are) were all wrong.

The next stage was to convince British and American publishers that Mozambican poetry was important, worthwhile or interesting. I'm afraid I didn't do a good job at convincing anyone because the response was usually that the poetry was "too strange" or "too exotic".

And so the years went by.

And in the meantime three of the poets included in the anthology passed on: José Craveirinha died in Johannesburg; Rui Knopfli and Noémia de Sousa died in Lisbon, where I was now living. Noémia had been called the 'mother of Mozambican poetry' and Rui and José were the two giants who had dominated Mozambican poetry for almost fifty years. The masters were dead—they weren't all dead, because Glória de Sant'Anna was still writing from her exile—and in many ways this signalled the end of an era.

The younger generations continued to write and publish. It did not make sense to make 1993/1994 the cut-off date for the anthology, and so I filled in the gaps, brought the anthology up to date. I toyed with the thought of rewriting the introduction, but I desisted from the idea, not because it reflected my thinking at the time and it is useful for that reason, but because I still hold by what I said back then.

At the time I was very intrigued with the connections with the East. There was the Goan connection: Mozambique began as a Goan dependency; Campos Oliveira (1847-1911), the first significant native-born Mozambican poet, was Goan; so many other 'black' poets had Goan ancestors (Rui de Noronha, for example). I was also fascinated with Islam, by its numerical strength and its influence on the cultural life of the north, and also the way Islam didn't really make its way into poetry, except, that is, for Knopfli's poems on the Island of Mozambique. There was also Hinduism, which appeared in Knopfli, but also in the work of Fonseca Amaral, a poet I had included in the first version of this anthology. And then there were Patraquim's prose-poems on the Island of Mozambique which came out in 1991; these poems reclaimed and rejoiced in the island's mixed heritage: Arabic and European, Islamic and Christian. I could see that the East was present in Mozambican poetry, but it wasn't one of the grand themes, but rather one of the many layers that went into the making up of Mozambican identity, one of the many substrata.

One of the interesting developments in Mozambican poetry over the last ten years has been a recuperation of the 'Oriental' and of Mozambique's Eastern heritage. Ana Mafalda Leite entitled one of her books *Rosas da China* (2000), which literally means 'Roses from China'; her subsequent book, *Passaporte do Coração* (2002), renders homage to Mozambique's Islamic legacy. Eduardo White's long prose-poem *Janela para Oriente* (1999) is a window to the Orient, a meditation on the East (India, China, Japan, Vietnam, the Philippines, Arabia, etc.) and what this East signifies to the poet. Rui Knopfli's last book, published just before he died, a book about the Mozambique of his childhood, was called *O Monhé das Cobras* (1997), which means something like 'The Indian Man with the Snakes'; it is interesting how Knopfli makes the most emblematic Mozambican figure (in the sense that he gives title to the book) an Indian snake-charmer . . . A recent longish poem (included in this anthology) by the unfaltering Glória de Sant'Anna recuperates Swahili, Arabic, and Malay aspects of Mozambique's coastal culture. (What would Craveirinha and Noémia de Sousa make of this? Well, perhaps if we re-read their work we will see that the tendency was already there.) How do we account for this convergence? To suggest that poets influenced each other seems too pat, especially when we know that poets were working independently, and that when they discovered similar things in each other's work they were both surprised and delighted. Perhaps this orientation towards the East is part of some sort of unconscious interpellation: they did not choose to look eastwards, but something in our time demanded that they look in that direction. This may have something to do with a wide angle view of history, with a sense of history as being longer than the colonial period. Equally, it might have something to do with revaluation of the living traditions in the country, the traditions of minority cultures and religions, and also the more obscure traditions that have long blended into black culture. What this eastward gaze also indicates is that the West does not have all the answers.

Acknowledgements

Different people have helped me at the different stages of making this selection of Mozambican poetry. Some helped me to find texts which had long been forgotten or were out of print or had never been published. Others read the translations, and others set up interviews with the poets or with the staff at the various archives. They took me into their homes, they were patient, hospitable and generous with their time. In particular, I thank the following people, in South Africa, in Portugal, and in Mozambique, most warmly for their efforts: Matteo Angius, Graham Bailey, the late Maria Emília Cerejo, Rose Cohen, Mia Couto, the late José Craveirinha, the late Amílcar Fernandes, Ana Mafalda Leite, Fátima Mendonça (then at the Universidade Eduardo Mondlane), Hélder Muteia, the late Glória de Sant'Anna, António Sopa, and the late Noémia de Sousa. I thank also my fellow-translators, Stephen Gray and Maria de Lourdes Magalhães for the many-many weekends which they dedicated towards this project.

I also wish to express my gratitude to the Ernest Oppenheimer Institute for Portuguese Studies at the University of the Witwatersrand, Johannesburg, which funded a research trip to Mozambique and contributed towards a similar trip to Portugal, without which I could not have acquired most of the important material in this book.

Finally I would like to thank the editors of *New Contrast*, *Staffrider*, *Envoi* and *Portuguese Studies* where versions of many of the translations first appeared:

New Contrast (*South African Literary Journal*): Luís Carlos Patraquim: "Metamorphosis", "I draw the curtains of the afternoon . . ."; Glória de Sant'Anna: "Sea", "Ever Since the World"; Rui Knopfli: "Green Mangoes with Salt"; José Craveirinha: "Elegy to my Grandmother Fanisse".

Staffrider: Noémia de Sousa: "Poem for Rui de Noronha"; Reinaldo Ferreira: "If I never said that your teeth . . . ", "Copélia"; Glória de Sant'Anna: "Drawing on the Sand", "Condition", "Nocturne", "Second Poem on Solitude"; José Craveirinha: "Land of Canaan", "Canticle of the Blue Bird in Sharpeville", "Communiqué from Cuíto Cuanavale"; Luís Carlos Patraquim: "I think of your hands as gills inside the sea . . . ", "Carnivorous Elegy"; Rui Knopfli: "Ariel's Song", "The Dog of Anguish".

Envoi: José Craveirinha: "Maria Sende", "Why? "; Glória de Sant'Anna: "Poem of the Sea", "The Elderly Fisherman", "Poem"; Luís Carlos Patraquim: "I think of your hands as gills inside the sea . . . ", "Carnivorous Elegy".

Portuguese Studies: José Craveirinha: "Black Outcry", "Mama Saquina", "Our City", and "Curse".

CAMPOS OLIVEIRA (1847 - 1911)

- *O Mancebo e Trovador Campos Oliveira* (1985) — a selection of his poetry

The significance of Campos Oliveira is primarily historical, for he was the first significant poet to have actually been born in Mozambique. A government clerk for most of his poet, he published widely in newspapers and magazines in Goa (Portuguese India), Portugal and Mozambique. He founded Mozambique's first literary magazine, *Revista Africana*. A selection of his poetry was edited by Manuel Ferreira, a Portuguese academic.

The Fisherman from Mozambique [4]
—1874

"I was born in Mozambique,[*]
my parents were humble people,
the black colour of their skin
is the same as mine:
I have been a fisherman since I was child,
and I have always roved the sea;
fishing is my livelihood,
and no other trade have I looked for.

You will find me by the shore
even before the sun has risen;
if I take time off to rest,
it does not mean I am lazy;
in my frail and light canoe,
always so far away from home,
I am at the mercy of the wind and the waves
and death I do not fear.

I go from Cabaceira[†] to the beaches,
I go all the way past Mussuril,
even if the sky is all gloom,
or if it's the colour of the indigo;
from Lumbo I set into the water
all the way to Sancul,
and soon I am in the high sea,
even if the north wind's blowing or the southerly's raging.

Only at night is the canoed moored,
so's to give my body a rest,
and to spend glad times
next to the woman I cherish:

---

[*] The island of Mozambique.
[†] Settlement on the mainland, opposite the Island of Mozambique.

26

a fisherman also needs
sweet caresses from his wife,
because the sorrows of this life
make one almost forget about love!

It's a sad thing when your life's
always in danger—how I know that!—
but if you put your faith in God
you won't fear the wrath of the sea;
it's a small reward
for a life as hard as this;
but as long as I don't die of hunger,
what does the rest matter?

I have been a fisherman since I was child,
and I have always roved the sea;
fishing is my livelihood,
and no other trade have I looked for;
and for as long as I have arms,
an oar and a canoe out there,
I'll always live happily
in this trade I have chosen!"

RUI DE NORONHA (1909 - 1943)

- *Sonetos* (1946)

Generally regarded as the 'founding father' of modern Mozambican poetry, Rui de Noronha's poetry was the first major articulation of an African 'cry of despair' at the injustices to which black Mozambicans were subjected. But if Rui de Noronha is to be regarded as Mozambique's proto-nationalist poet, this must be qualified with the angst and ambivalence that permeates his poetry, and which points to a more ambiguous relationship with the colonial society which both co-opted him and excluded him. He published widely in newspapers, including *O Brado Africano*, the early black nationalist newspaper. His only book of poetry, *Sonetos* [Sonnets], was published posthumously. His use of the sonnet form was the inheritance of Portuguese Romanticism, and his language was dated even as he wrote.

Rise Up and Walk [5][*]
—1936

You sleep! and the word marches ahead, O nation of mystery.
You sleep! and the world moves in orbit, the world moves on . . .
On one hemisphere Progress walks to the summit
On the other you sleep your never-ending slumber . . .

The jungle becomes your sinister and solitary abode
Where at night the lone beast is roaring. . .
Time hurls strange curses in your face[†]
And you, O Africa, estranged from Time, sleeping . . .

Arise. Already the black crows are flapping in the sky
Eager to descend and gulp down
The warm blood of your sleep-walking flesh.

Arise. So much sleep is not of this world.
Listen to the voice of Progress, this other Nazarene,
Who offers his hand and says, "Africa, rise up and walk!"

---

[*] "Then Peter said, Silver and gold have I none; but such as I have I give thee: In the
name of Jesus Christ of Nazareth rise up and walk" (Acts 3.6 King James Version).
[†] This version of the sonnet, the original one, differs from the better-known one
which appeared in the posthumous *Sonetos* (1943).

REINALDO FERREIRA (1922 - 1959)

- *Poemas* (1960)

The poet was held in high regard during his lifetime, even by the members of the colonial-bourgeois society he scorned and despised. He contributed widely to various journals and newspapers, and a year after his death a group of friends and admirers collected many of his poems in a book simply entitled *Poemas* [Poems]. Written from within both the European modernist and Romantic traditions, his poetry uses those very traditions to demystify the tropics. Reinaldo Ferreira's poetry is not 'typically' African. But that is also one of the dangers of defining African poetry within the parameters of purely nationalist concerns.

Rome A.D. 476 [6]

To be a barbarian is to be pure; the blood's new and strong;
It's the russet and the brutal which herald
The golden decadence; it's the Spring
within the hypnotic Autumn of death.

When the goblets cannot hold any more wine
And the hand which has poured it already shakes,
The barbaric impulse which alters the equilibrium
Is russet and it comes from the north.

Oh! And we whose vicious and refined
Days have already been counted!
Rain on, triumphantly, petals, carnations,

As if asking for the ultimate orgy!
For perhaps before the new day is born
From the north they will come and make us into slaves . . .

"If I never said that your teeth . . ." [7]

If I never said that your teeth
Are pearls,
It's because they are teeth.
If I never said that your lips
Are red corals,
It's because they are lips.
If I never said that your eyes
Are onyx, or emeralds, or sapphires,
It's because they are eyes.
Pearls and onyx and corals are things,
And things don't exalt things.
If someday in some vague place
I were to praise you,
I surely would search in poetry,
In the landscape and in the music,
For the unsurpassable images
Of the eyes and the lips and the teeth.
But believe me, believe me in all sincerity,
That metaphors are worthless
To express that which I see.
And I see lips, eyes, teeth.

"When the façades, tomb-like . . ." [8]

When the façades, tomb-like and speckled with grey,
Suggest that indifference to falling asleep
I am set free into uncharted worlds—
And the night is an ally to the fantasies in my attic . . .

Slender and red-haired—a whole sky of freckles—
He has that alluring nakedness of those who can't be possessed . . .
Perhaps I am a painter of horrid nudes,
I scoff at the Masters and despise all uniforms!

But as soon as the cold and sterile brightness appears
—For the dawn always obstructs
The quick and imminent encounter—

I begin to be afraid of my nocturnal self,
My affinity with a folly that my
More chaste self has repudiated!

"Coffee-bars on the quay . . ." [9]
—1952

Coffee-bars on the quay
where all the equally anonymous
meet each other,
the rats in the holds,
the Babel of all slanderous words,
river of smoke and unrestrained rut,
over-sexed river
that seeks the one single sea,
women to sleep the night,
anoint yourself with disgust
for you are no Amphitrite,[*]
flimsy maritime fantasy,
but the loathsome
and ever-protective
familiar shade
of the Virgin of Vice,
Our Lady of the Lower World.

---

[*] Venus, especially in her manifestation as goddess of the sea.

Coppélia [10]

From Coppélia I keep three sadly wistful letters,
a ribbon, and a rose,
a faintly discoloured bud
which took its fragrance from her locks.
An elusive air, both ancient and sad,
permeates the place.
But Coppélia doesn't exist of course
and neither do the letters.
She is real to be me because she is absent,
and because I never possessed her
I trust both in my vision of her
and in the memory of who she was in my past,
in the clandestine walks we took,
in the stars we made, in some kiss we shared,
in the exaltation of some dance that floated away,
in the feeling that a cloud was weaving itself around me;
and in the smooth, pure and fine emotion
of that time when her hand
delayed itself next to mine.
This is Coppélia,
if by chance it was her destiny
to have been born or to have lived,
to have been refused to me by a stern father,
and to whom I would have dedicated ill-fitting poems
without ever having possessed her,
so she, belonging to another
or having died a virgin,
could remain, clear and alive,
within me.

Notes

Rome A.D. 476. The oppression of the African majority and the silencing and political repression that went with living in a police state were like bombs ready to be detonated. The poets of Mozambique were quite sensitive to the inevitable outcome. Even when the poets were not nationalist—in the sense that Craveirinha was—they were nevertheless aware that something terrible was going to happen. Rome in the year 476, where the date represents the year when the Barbarians overran the Western Roman Empire, is a metaphor for Mozambique. The metaphor, as with any metaphor, should not be taken too literally, and in particular the line "From the north they will come and make us into slaves . . .". The colonial war was to start in the north (no less than four years after the poet had died), but that is as far as we can take the comparison. Yet Reinaldo Ferreira's preoccupations were prophetic. The idea that colonial Mozambique was living the heady days of its "golden decadence" before the crash is certainly correct. Readers familiar with the work of Kavafis—a poet from another 'African' sea-port, in this case Alexandria—will also recognize preoccupations not too dissimilar from those found in his "Waiting for Barbarians".

"If I never said that your teeth . . ." This poem is frequently anthologised; it often appears in textbooks and readers for primary-school children. It is a deceptively simple poem, but it asks important questions about the nature of artistic convention. For example, convention has it that teeth should be compared to pearls—such as we get in the expression 'pearly white teeth'. But just because pearls are the most natural metaphor for white teeth does not mean that the metaphor is anything else other than 'convention'. This poem is a good introduction into the way Ferreira subtly subverts and undermines certain conventional notions.

"When the façades, tomb-like and speckled with grey . . ." Verbs in Portuguese do not require a subject pronoun; for example, I do not need to write 'he sings', it is sufficient for me to say 'sings' for the reader to know that it is he that sings. In the original, the line beginning with the words "He has that alluring nakedness . . ." does not have the pronoun 'he'; but neither does it have 'she'. Extra-textual information would suggest that the object of desire is a he; Reinaldo Ferreira never denied the fact that he was attracted to men. What is interesting in the poem is not the fact of this, but the dual sense of attraction and turning away from the object of his desire: the poet-narrator hates what he has relished in the night before. But a repudiation of this 'base love' is precisely the sort of conventional end that tradition would have demanded of the poem.

Nocturnal Song. The poem is a hymn to the "Virgin of Vice, Our Lady of the Underworld". This inversion of familiar patterns, this travesty of bourgeois convention, is of course reminiscent of Genet. This was not the respectable urban world of the white bourgeoisie; this was the underworld, the dark world of nightlife and of forbidden passions. Ferreira sings about what few other Mozambican poet have sung about: the pick-up joints by the harbour.

Coppélia. This is a very camp poem about a love affair with an imaginary lady perhaps named after the heroine in Leo Delibes's ballet *Coppélia*. The poet describes Coppélia in the language of pure romanticism: the diction is elevated and the images suggest a melancholy surfeit, an excess of love and longing. But this edifice is raised up only in order to be toppled down with the revelation that Coppélia does not actually exist. Real women do not exist in this poetry; they function merely as aspects of a convention, as signs pointing to something else.

JOSÉ CRAVEIRINHA (1922 - 2003)

- *Chigubo* (1964), reprinted as *Xigubo* (1980)
- *Karingana ua Karingana* (1974)
- *Cela 1* (1980)
- *Maria* (1988)
- *Babalaze das Hienas* (1997)
- *Maria* (1998) — enlarged edition
- *Obra Poética I* (1999) — the first part of his collected works
- *Poemas de Prisão* (2003)

Without doubt one of the most important poets writing in Portuguese in the last century, José Craveirinha gave the Portuguese tradition(s) a poetic corpus born out of the African experience. His is a lyricism where the social is carefully interconnected with the private; his poetic diction, as much as it uses, as it does in his famous poems of outrage and denunciation, the full range or inherited rhetorical devices, is often devoid of any ornamentation; at the same time, his poetry is noted for its dazzling metaphors, where the bold fusion of apparently unusual elements or concepts gives his great hymns of hope and indignation a great and visionary clarity. Craveirinha's handling of the Portuguese language cannot be faulted, and he belongs to a tradition of great Portuguese poets like Luís de Camões; at the same time, his use of an African-derived syntax, African-inflected neologisms, and imagery derived from a specifically African worldview, all work at producing a poetic language that is both traditional and innovative, simultaneously Portuguese and Mozambican. Appropriately enough, in 1991 he was awarded the *Prémio Camões*, the highest literary accolade in the Luso-Afro-Brazilian world of Portuguese-speakers. Much of Craveirinha's poetry remains uncollected, however.

For most of his life he worked as a journalist. Between 1965 and 1969 he was imprisoned by the PIDE, the security police of Portugal's fascist regime. He was president of the Mozambican Writers' Association (AEMO) between 1982 and 1987. In 1983 he was awarded the Lotus Prize by the Association of Afro-Asian Writers. José Craveirinha died in Johannesburg, South Africa

Hope [11]
—1945-50

The agama* lizard
in the marula tree
darts its blue head.

The spider weaves
its kanga of cobwebs
in the purple attics
of twilight.

And as for us?
Ah, we wait
in the euphoria of our sweating backs
for the salt of piled-up injuries
to be obliterated.

---

* The Southern tree agama (*agama atricollis*), a lizard common all over Southern
Africa, is distinguished by its cobalt-blue head.

The Pores of the Plague [12]
—1945-50

The
cat fattened with blood
listening to the mother-of-pearl of the nails
sadly hears the African rumble
of our stitched-up khaki skin
chirping with the noise
of heaps of emerging rats,
the lost heads
in the million pores
of the plague!

Fable [13]
—1945-50

Fat boy bought a balloon
and blew
he blew the yellow balloon with lotsa strength.

Fat boy blew
blew
blew
the balloon filled up
filled up
and burst open!

Thin boys picked up the scraps
and made small balloons.

Civilization [14]
—1945-50

In ancient times
(before the time of Jesus)
men erected temples and stadiums
and died in the arena like dogs.

Now . . .
they're making Cadillacs as well.

Oh! Carmen de Diego [15]
—1957

How I could feel your Spain on the day we discovered each other, Carmen!

Somewhere on that day in Cordoba or Andalusia
somewhere on that day, who was it who profaned your virginity,
burnt your smile in the bombed-out barn in San Sebastian
and pasted the walls of Madrid with the newspaper ends
of the fragments of people's bodies,
manifestoes of the agony of workers and farmers
in the swastika-filled labour posters
where women and children
laid out a carpet for the graceful lizards
of Mussolini's tanks to trample them over
until the waters of the Guadalquivir
were reddened with unreachable screams?
Who was it, Carmen?

Oh! Carmen de Diego!
Oh! The sinister footsteps of the Falange![*]
Oh! The sinister eyes of the Legion![†]
Oh! The *malagueñas*[‡] of horror in the smoky remains of homes!
Oh! The deadly speedwells of the fast fascist Fiats in Barcelona!
Oh! The Messerschmidt hogs festering the proletarian blue of Saragossa's sky!
Oh! The Stukkas of prey laying rotten eggs over Guernica!
Oh! Our brothers shot by firing-squads in the hills of Guadarrama!
Oh! Our lovely young girls—raped and killed in Oviedo!
Oh! The bombs from the Junker fighters, the men and the mothers!
        the girls
        the young men and the mothers!

---

[*] The Falange (lit. Phalanx) Party, the rightwing totalitarian organization that fought the civil war against the leftwing Republicans, and which governed Spain between 1939 and 1975.

[†] The fascist 'Condor Legion'.

[‡] The *malagueña* is a Spanish folk-dance from Malaga.

Oh! The sadistic mortal sluggishness of the Hitlerian armoured tanks!
. . . the Hitlerian armoured tanks
trampling the heart of the Spanish people.
Oh! The mortars harvesting the vineyards of Malaga, most
unagronomically!

Oh, twenty one years after the ash of the lurid grenades
and I still breathe into your loose black hair, Carmen!
I still feel the nightmare heave up in your breasts, Carmen!
I still see the fear in your Iberian eyes, Carmen!
I still sob in your sobbing red lips, Carmen!
I, José, kiss your kisses that kiss me, Carmen!
I, the suffering of Carmen de Diego!
suffering . . .
suffering . . .
I, enraged, crying out: Carmen de Diego
crying . . .
crying!!!

Oh! The civil war decimating the good people of Spain!
Oh! Carmen of the bloodied ruins of your city of San Sebastian!
Oh! My Carmen de Diego, compatriot of Federico García Lorca!
Oh! My Carmen de Diego, fellow-countrywoman of *ñuestra companera*
. . . our comrade Dolores La Pasionaria![§]

Ah! The vultures of Spain turned against the martyred people of Spain!
Ah! The castanets of bullets for you to dance to,
anguished with your mantilla
. . . For you to dance to with your mantilla covered in blood
and acrid with gunpowder
. . . The bloodied gypsy dance
of your agony in a Catalonian night
In a Catalonian night
the bloodied gypsy dance
of a life that's ever more alive
in the midst of so much death!

[§] Dolores Ibarruri, La Pasionaria or 'The Passion Flower', Communist leader and
one of the important figures on the Republican side during the Spanish civil war.

Ah! For the genuine *fandangos*[**] of Spain's future barricades!
Ah! And tomorrow, Carmen, the victory of our slaughtered brothers!
Ah! Carmen de Diego!
Ah! Carmen de Diego!
Ah! Carmen de Diego
you and I both countryless,
both of us imprisoned in the exile of each other's arms,
liberating your own Spain, from the Pyrenees to the Mediterranean,
and all the land of Monomotapa's[††] former empire
we will also liberate,
my Mozambique!

[**] A lively dance from southern Spain; it is danced with castanets.
[††] Monomotapa was an ancient Southern African empire whose land area included most of what is modern-day Zimbabwe and Mozambique.

45

When José Thinks of America [16]
—1958

Letter to Doreen Martin

Doreen,
In Mafalala* when José thinks of America
he does not envy a single of Manhattan's skyscrapers,
the spectacular billboards of Broadway don't dazzle José,
and neither is José much convinced by the feats of Popeye the Sailor Man
after he's consumed a tin of publicity spinach.
In Mafalala when José thinks of America
the memory-filled ancient tears of negro spirituals
add salt to the dirty tarred roads of the great Mississippi,
and a shoot-out in a lively central avenue in Chicago
does not respect the shirt of the factory worker
who'd been to buy a coke at the supermarket during his tea-break,
and then they expect José to admire
the modernist architecture of Chicago,
when now and then he gets thinking, for example,
about what purpose a dozen new Packards serve
for the two hundred million Americans
in the thousand-and-one highways of America.

In the true-life fables
of places like New Orleans and Harlem,
steps in Louis Armstrong and
steps out Jesse Owens.
Steps in Joe Louis and
steps out Marian Andersen.
Steps in Duke Ellington and
steps out Lena Horne.
Steps in Paul Robeson and
steps out Richard Wright with his five hundred
thousand families including José's own family,
and while Duke Ellington resolves
a series of abstract jazz problems

---

* Peri-urban area in Lourenço Marques (now Maputo) where the poet lived.

46

with his piano
an obscene Cadillac of a lascivious blue
exhibits its shiny chromium plate
with thanks to General Motors.

So!
Doreen, it's mere fortuitousness
the way all this coincides:
between the firm principles of the White House,
a few tons of chewing gum packets,
hands clapping at Nat King Cole's voice
and at his defrizzed hair,
and the visual effects of the wild paint strokes of the police truncheons
democratically painting
the sweat of blacks the colour red.

And
it's more or less an abstract question
but the children who are forcibly born in Xipamanine[†]
or those who play in the non-luxurious rubbish of Harlem
when they can speak for themselves
they'll shout in our faces that it's the exact opposite
even if a special agent hears them in New York
and reports it back to certain officials in LM.[‡]

Now, my friend Doreen,
now that José has seen with his own eyes
for a whole twelve months
Marilyn with nothing but a smile to cover her up,
the whole of her, from her toenails right up to her hair,
exposed in colour so as to warm and warm
the twelve pages of the calendar,
in truth José admires Donald Duck much more
in truth José prefers Laurel & Hardy much more
in truth José appreciates much more Mickey Mouse
and what's more José honestly has more sympathy

[†] Xipamanine was a slum-type residential area on the outskirts of Lourenço Marques (now Maputo).

[‡] Lourenço Marques was also known as 'LM'.

with the implausible philosophy of the Marx Brothers
when he listens to the ancestral dialects of the 'rhythm'
beating out the metallic sorcery of the 'blues'
the eyes sunken in like the ones of those who are stoned
after their fifteenth joint when fear doesn't mean anything
and beholds the new dogma
of sprinters arriving at number one
or two gloved men defining the ideology of the knockout
or, still, discovering the magical revelation of books
with the grandparents and grandchildren
in the paradises of mineral ore
with the parents and daughters
in the joy of the cotton fields
all of them together in the corner of the word a step away from the beautiful
jukebox cheaply playing
"Made in the United States of America!"
when they insert a mere cent in the slot.

And in the midst of all of this, Doreen
there comes out a terrible feminine photo
publicly confidential
who turns out to be none other than Marilyn Monroe
a star full of potential
but when José from Mafalala thinks of America
it's not by chance that he doesn't think of Marilyn's potential
for showing everyone the logic of profit
of the methods of propaganda that Americans
use . . . *usa* . . . USA !!!

But do you know what, Doreen,
a thick shadow of people shuffle their feet sluggishly
by the third streetlight of a road, in front of a police station
and José remembers that Jesse Owens made it to the Olympics
and, against all odds, won four gold medals
and do you know where that took place? Right inside Hitler's armoured
                                                                    heart

And what's more,
José also remembers the revenge of Joe Louis

who KO-ed Max Schmeling[§] right in the first round
that when Armstrong blows his trumpet
the treble is the conclusive answer
to the sentimental doubts of the Ku-Klux-Klan
and Charlie Chaplin's rhetorical pair of boots

And to end off this letter, Doreen,
the members of the Klan may get angry with me
but they more or less already know most of what
José thinks to himself here in Mafalala
when José thinks of the blonde Marilyn Monroe
North America's pauper millionaire
all naked
giving others time off their insomnias
the whole year round.

[§] A German boxer from the Nazi period, the World Heavyweight Champion from
1930 to 1932. He was ignominiously defeated in a match against Joe Louis (1938).

Maria Sende [17]
—1958

There was the wind over the heads of wheat
there was rain over the river water
and over the heads of men there were
the caresses of fire from the *sjambok**

And in Africa's long night
there were
lost souls athirst for life
songs ululating the suffering
hands hardened by masturbating the spades
and mouths crazed by the screams
of the *xigubo*![†]

And the two of us, Maria Sende,
man and woman in this morning of all origins,
together in the spiral of a
black and white
raceless
dream!

---

* *SA Eng*, a whip made of animal hide, usually from the hippopotamus.
† *Xi-Ronga*, a praise dance performed before or after a battle.

Black Outcry [18]

I am coal!
Brutally you wrench me from the ground
And you make me your mine
Boss!

I am coal!
And you ignite me, boss
To serve you always as your driving force
But not for ever
Boss!

I am coal!
I have to burn, yes
And scorch all with my burning strength.

I am coal!
I have to burn while I'm exploited
Burn down to cursed ashes
Burn alive like my Brother the tar
Until I'm your mine no longer
Boss!

I am coal!
I have to burn
And scorch all with the burning of my fire.

Yes!
I will be your coal
Boss!

[Translated with Stephen Gray]

Curse 19

. . . But put in the hands of Africa your left-over bread
and for your gluttony I'll give you what's over from Mozambique's hunger
and you'll see how the nothing which I return
from my banquet of left-overs also fills you

As I see it,
all the bread you give
is everything you reject, O Europe!

[Translated with Stephen Gray]

Poem of a Future Citizen [20]

I have come from all the parts
of a Nation yet to be.
I have come and here I am!

I wasn't born as myself alone
neither were you nor anyone else . . .
but as a Brother.

But
I have love to give to the clench-handed.
Love being what I am
and nothing else.

And
I have in my heart
screams which are not only mine
because I come from a Country yet to be.

Ah! being what I am
I have Love to give to all.
I!
Every man
a citizen of a Nation yet to be.

[Translated with Stephen Gray]

Boat Song ²¹

If you were to see me die
the millions of times that I was born

If you were to see me cry
the millions of times you laughed . . .

If you were to see me shout
the millions of times I kept quiet . . .

If you were to see me sing
the millions of times I died
and bled . . .

I tell you, my European brother
you would be born
you would cry
you would sing
you would shout

And you would suffer
and bleed
millions of deaths like me!!!

[Translated with Stephen Gray]

Canticle of the Blue Bird in Sharpeville [22]
—1960

Thin men like myself
don't ask to be born
or to sing.
But they are born and they sing
because ours is the incorruptible voice
of the dragged-out steps taken in ancient plots
and the anguish that has no voice.

And if they sing and continue to be born,
thin men like myself with deep black rings under the eyes,
it wasn't as if we asked for the blasphemy
of a sun that wasn't the same
for a black child
as for an Afrikaner boy.

But we are all alike,
we share that same extraordinary delight
at the children we create.
Here we are,
with that vigorous desire
to live out the song we know well
and to change our lives
the life of 'volunteer'* we never asked for
and which we don't want
and despise,
from the African cotton we're forced to wear
to the ration of *mealie pap*† with which we're fed.

And with the seeds of the Ronga,
with the wild flowers on the hills of the Zulus,
and the dose of pollen

---

* A 'volunteer' to work on the mines, i.e., a forced recruit.
† *SAfr Eng*, maize meal or porridge.

from the machine-guns in the Sharpeville sky
a blue bird sings in the arms of a baobab
and in the sorceries of these skies
it shall raise the terrible voluptuousness of our flight.

Elegy to My Grandmother Fanisse [23]

Fanisse was my grandmother
and the shadow of the marula trees in the sand path
reminds me of the old kanga of striped calico
and the peanuts and ripe maize
in the plantation of Michafutene
two shouts away from the truck-filling station.

Fanisse was born like this in my mulatto eyes
and that's the way she remained through to old age
sweet potato   cashew-nut
mat under the mango tree
story of the clever rabbit told around the fire-side
the ritual prayer in the language of Mahazul[*]
and in the place where the heart is
the great moon.

Was nobody getting cross with grandmother Fanisse
was nobody spitting at the fate of Fanisse
was nobody stealing manioc
was nobody giving hiding
was nobody killing Fanisse?

Portuguese man was opening a road in the plantation
This Thorneycroft hooter in the distance
was giving this fright to baby goat of old Mabota
this small bird with this red beak
was running away!

Nobody was spitting
nobody was giving this hiding to grandma Fanisse
nobody was killing . . .
nobody was doing no such bad things.

---

[*] The name of one of the famous chiefs who resisted Portuguese incursions into Mozambican territory in the nineteenth century.

But that's how it was
that my grandma Fanisse
died!

Mama Saquina [24]

In the city
dazzling and unreal
the sorcery of it all
gripped Mama Saquina's heart
when she cried out:
"Go well, my João."

The train remained with Mama Saquina
in that memory wrapped
in a song of steel against steel
to the beat of João Tavasse went in the mines[*]
João Tavasse-went-in-the-mines
João Tavasse-went-in-the-mines
João Tavasse-went-in-the-mines

(On that morning, golden on the leaves of the cashew,
João Tavasse gone write at Commissioner)

And Mama Saquina
stayed on the land of Chibuto
with Mama Rosalina and old Massingue
with ten hectares of plain
for the seeds of the landlord
to fall on the land
and flower.

And night and day
the soul of Mama Saquina
clothed in a kanga of nightmares
cast itself on the ten blossoming hectares

(And João Tavasse never
return at Commissioner)

---

[*] The gold mines of the Witwatersrand, in South Africa.

And when the migrants' train let off steam
and pulled out,
the voice of its pistons sang:
João-Tavasse-went-in-the-mines
João-Tavasse-went-in-the-mines
João-Tavasse-went-in-the-mines

Mama Saquina carries the child on her back,
tears the maize from the soil
and makes a miracle of a hundred and fifty
bails of cotton!

[Translated with Stephen Gray]

I Want To Be a Drum

The drum's become old crying out
O ancient God of mankind
let me be a drum
only a drum crying into the hot tropical night.

And not a flower born in the bushveld of despair.
Not even a river running into the sea of despair.
Not even an assegai hardened by the live fire of despair.
Not even poetry forged in the ruddy pain of despair

Nothing at all!

Just a drum that's become old crying out at the full moon of my land
Just a cow-hide drum tanned under the sun of my land
Just a drum carved from the hard trunks of my land

Me!
Just a drum shattering the bitter silence of Mafalala.*
Just a drum that's become old bleeding in the *batuque*† of my people
Just a drum lost in the darkness of the lost night

O ancient God of mankind
I want to be a drum.
And not a river
not a flower
not an assegai—for now—
not even poetry

Only a drum echoing the song of life and strength
a drum all day and night
day and night only a drum
until the fulfilment of the great festivities of the *batuque*!

---

* Peri-urban area in Lourenço Marques (now Maputo) where the poet lived.
† *Xi-Ronga*, a cow-hide drum and/or a dance where drums predominate.

Oh, ancient God of mankind
let me be a drum
just a drum!

Martin Luther King [26]
—c. 1968

For the life he barely lived in the United States
and for the martyr's death they gave him in Memphis
I suspect that in two or three centuries' time
Martin Luther King
will have languid blue eyes
long blond hair
a white Nordic complexion
and God's surname.

It's bad enough that Jesus Christ
is no longer enough for them.

And in those days to come
how much will death's sting
from the wasp of lead
be worth?

Cell Number One [27]

—c. 1965-9

Here I am
as burnt-out
as a mad dog
licking the salty crust
of old wounds

In what language
and with what kind of face
will I tell my children
orphaned of a father
to forget everything?

Metamorphosis ²⁸

—c. 1965-9

During the nights
my hand which sculpts shapes
is a thought made naked.

Over the last two years
my fingers which have changed into the shape
of Sophia Loren or Claudia Cardinale
have—with voluptuousness—betrayed
only Ava Gardner, my former beloved,
a name I won't mention,
and my wife, Maria.

[Translated with Stephen Gray]

Wax-Shine [29]
—c. 1965-9

The old hyena
with blood-gleaming eyes
serves me the kidneys of anguish
and with her vile teeth,
flesh-eating,
she gnaws at the unbreakable marrow of the dream.

And within the four sides
of the fascist horizon of walls
—the precise dimensions of a coffin—
are the inevitable paces of someone
who has been cloistered.

And life
whose outrages have been hard-swallowed
has the taste of the slobber of howling hyenas
and while on a day of dismal sun
the acacias at least still cry out their flowers,
fear, kneeling on all fours,
is drawing wax-shine from the city.

Our City [30]
—1972

Our city
bizarre in this bilharzia of long nights
tamed like pet cats that purr
at their owners' feet and over the half-opened stone thighs
on the sheet of the city dwellers
like a woman gratified for the second time.

And on the islands
of the city the godforsaken kids
with faces tattooed in dry snot
all like catapulted birds in the cashews of all wickedness
all with the yellow eyes of the faraway eggnog of an African sun
all in living flesh without the sulphur of a morsel of bread
all of them with the cashew-nut that is chewed by the cannibalistic
[molars of the road.

Our city,
cemetery for those who are dead before their time
and a desert peopled by José the mulatto, jeep of caresses
over the naked knees of girls hungry also for
the anguish of sexual desire
females and males seized by idleness
devouring themselves between rumours and football reports
or transforming the car bought on instalments into their universe and
cloister
the clenched teeth of those who strum the guitars
in the rhythms of alarm from the core of the stonework,
but how much does it cost, after all
how much does it cost, the measure of peanuts
of the black boy with his face tattooed
in dry snot?

[Translated with Stephen Gray]

67

Excerpt from an Autograph Book for a Vietnamese Child [31]

I

Gillette razors
which in their euphoria have us drawn and quartered
with the tenderness of their adjectives of steel
and through the A + B of the agrarian theories of the B52s
wisdom is scattered over the swamps
where women and children thought they were
performing the age-old agricultural fable
called rice-paddy.

Now we're all doing
the yoga of the bombs
we've all been shelved away in some philosophy of 'redundancies'
which includes spinal columns
and skulls
and even ploughs which oxidize in the sun
because with the Made-in-the-USA screams of the missiles
no one can hear the old concepts of Vietnamese agronomy
which are unable to plead and thus have to modernize themselves
in the scrap heap.

II

They move Biblically,
in the Exodus of the chosen,
in this dust from craters which had once been roads
that led to the village celebrating the harvest,
and at times they all seem like bare shadows,
yet liable to real tricks
such as smouldering arms of burnt rubber waving a last goodbye
or the sight of children leaving the rubble
to join in the solemn prayers of the monks.

And hissing yataghans
arising from the quiver of the alluring night
kindle the hidden designs
of *Xicuembo**
and Buddha.

---

* *Xi-Ronga*, God or gods or spirits from the other world.

extracts from **The Tasty Tanjarines of Inhambane** [32]
—1982-84

I
Doesn't the clapping of hands
that applauds the speeches of those in authority
have any doubts at all?
Aren't certain excessive eulogies,
all filled with 'Vivas!'* quite fraudulent?
Let us prick our ears with careful attention
at the shrieking shouts at meetings.
And what about the overflowing queues?
Isn't the hidden whispering quite bizarre?

In their epics of humility
they should at least leave the dreamers intact.
Sabotage is to demote a real poet to the status of a clerk.
Aren't there enough incompetent people in the offices already?
Are more carpets and air conditioners still needed?

Let us keep the crafty diagrams for the top brass.
Notice the skilful reports of the state companies
prospering in deficit either because of the drought
or because newspapers said it rained too much
or because of the sun
or because there is a screw missing in the tractor
or perhaps because a traffic cop didn't fine Vasco da Gama
for transgressing the traffic regulations of Calicut's spice route

And what about the circles of whispers at our eardrums?
Isn't it 'good ideology' to ascertain the origins
of all 'unquestionable' rumours?
Isn't a silenced population a security risk?
Where do they hide the full range of their voices?

---

* 'Viva', lit. 'Long Live', was a common struggle slogan, both in Mozambique and in
South Africa.

And what about the mutism of the makers of poesy?
No poetry comes out of it,
or do you think the rosy promised end
will rise out of summer twilights in shanty towns?
Who is the mega-star in the weather forecast of unfortunate news?
Who heeds to the signs of the wind before the thunderstorm
and gives warning?

II
From the sides of the road tarred with rubbish
let us gaze, puzzled,
at the sarcastic-looking buildings we have smashed up.
Doesn't it hurt?
Is it *very much better* to break up school desks
and crawl on the floor to study?
And in the factories what hands are these,
these proletarian hands of ours,
that when they work only de-factorize?
And what goes with the fattened-up responsible director
always sending himself on work missions
to the best hotels in Eastern and Western Europe?
And what about the full bag of the night-watchman's spoils,
is the nation's shortage worth more than having belonged to the [PIDE,[†]
is it worth more or isn't it, Fakir, my clever militiaman?

[Translated with Maria de Lourdes Magalhães]

[†] Acronym for 'International Police for State Security', the Portuguese security police
during the time of the fascist dictatorship.

71

Land of Canaan [33]
—1982

No, Israeli pilot, no.
It's pointless to look for the beautiful words of the *Song of Songs*
in the raging fires of Beirut
and in the innocent bodies mutilated
by burning shell splinters.

Fly closer to the ground.
Swiftly descend in your fighter-bomber.
Fly closer to the ground. Fly closer still, Hebrew pilot.
Fly towards Eichmann.[*] Fly to the depths of self-loathing.
Speed up until you and the motors and the match-stick bombs
eagerly kiss the sacred ground.

Was it for this Holocaust you survived
your own genocide in the days of Nazi-land?
Is this your long-desired Land of Canaan?
Do you really think this is the way you will attain peace
in the Promised Land?

---

[*] Adolf Eichmann (1906-1962), an SS Lieutenant-Colonel, was Chief of the Jewish
Office of the Gestapo during World War II and implemented the 'Final Solution'
which aimed at the total extermination of the Jewish people. On 2 December 1961
he was sentenced to death for crimes against the Jewish people and for crimes against
humanity.

Necklaces [34]
—1987

To Winnie Mandela,
my sister over there.

In the mythical times of Jupiter
vengeance was the nectar of the gods.

In these unreal times of *Boere**
no kind of revenge
should be allowed to taint the suffering souls
of those with a just cause.

It's obvious that Jupiter in his Olympian heights
and the *Boere* on the outskirts of Soweto
look somewhat implausible as gods
especially when the pharynxes that glow in the rubber tyre
necklaces are those of our brothers.

---

* *SA Eng/Afk*, Afrikaners or, by extension, supporters of the apartheid regime.

Why? [35]
—1987

A troubled sky bereft of clouds
spread over the townships
and hanging over the cities.

But . . .
why gross Firestone neckbands
why the rank smell of GoodYear collars
to add a final touch
to the ceremonious attire
of robot men
set on fire?

I know that my friend Nelson
is just as averse as I am
to the pyrotechnics
of that pungent smell
of an after-shave of burning rubber
that melts the closely shaved neck
for once and for all
into a black pitch.

So, why
my sister Winnie?

My sister Winnie
why?

Communiqué from Cuíto Cuanavale [36]
—c. 1988

To Jacinto, Luandino, Pepetela, David Mestre and Mitó, whom I dedicate this humble attempt of mine to be closer to them in that place where they are most at.

Your José embraces you.

I
Under the throttled skies of Cubango-Cubango
foul birds with cancerous eggs
search in vain
to give play to their drunken lunacy
over the holy ground of Cuíto Cuanavale.

The vile praetorian Impalas* have been detonated,
just as they were in the days of Shaka.
The great ancestral blood
of the land
cannot be vanquished.

II
How fortunate is the destiny of the Afrikaner kid
who delights in his own ideological suicide
in the Mirage that traps him
in the laughter
of its flames?

III
Isn't it one more soldier
who will never walk the streets of Hillbrow†
in civvies?

---

* Impala fighter jets.
† High-rise suburb in Johannesburg famed, at the time, for its night- life.

Or is it an unavoidable Afrikaner fate,
a Rand Show[‡] of last rites,
a typical Springbok spree,
a funeral-service picnic
on the pastures of Cuíto?

IV
Was it so they could keep vigil
over their son's coffin
that the parents of the fallen pilot
gave their vote
in support of a dogma
fit for Satan?

Or was it for the grieved to file past
under the anguished strains of bugles
and under the reverberating echoes
of the un-exultant and customary
salvoes of funerals?

Is it merely to earn an extra bier
that, in the absence of Mandela,
the Mirages and their rockets
defile the ground of Angola?

Questions this missive asks with indignation.
But let no one reply.
It's unnecessary.

In Cuíto Cuanavale
the dead reply
with all the strength of life!

[‡] A reference to the Rand Agricultural Show, South Africa's largest trade fair.

Memento 37
—1988

Over and above the heroic symbols we all have
each citizen in his own country
has his own
heroes or deities.

I am one of these citizens.
You are the person in question.*

And also the friends who wouldn't greet you
during my imprisonment
and all the neighbours who turned their faces
and the officials who interrogated me,
they all know your rightful place.

---

* The poet's deceased wife, Maria.

Hyenas and Gashes[38]

The inhuman
gashes of flesh
From
A thousand cutlasses.

Razor-sharp
Lips
In whose blood
The tongue is un-licked.

Hyenas
In the single-mindedness
Of their banquets
In the slaughter-houses.

The gashes
Eternal dogmas
In the deaths of this spree
And
You don't know
Half of it, Maria!

De Profundis 39

An open day cold with the clouds
On the bough the small birds of
sorrow
Warbling tears. A
Perfumed
Armful
Of crowns
From the depths.

So hard
So terse
Our goodbye of roses, Maria

De Profundis [40]

Possessed by blood
In the 'I will not turn again'
Of screams

In the snarls
Of the rabble
In a *De profundis* of knives.

Burnt Down Village [41]

But
it is on those nights
when the stars have been fumigated
that the hyenas
operate.

It's
ash
what's left over of the huts.

Gluttony [42]

The insidious hyenas
howl
their curses
their own wrath.

Rituals
of such gross gluttony
that even it comes to the famished
villagers of the tragedy
the gluttony of the hyenas
makes the cutlasses
the axes
slobber with anticipation

Barber's Shop 43

In the barber's shop in the dark
Júlio Chaúque was shaved
when he returned from the *mealie** plantation.

The ones who saw it
said that Júlio was shaved very closely
with plain bush knives
pretending to be Gillette razors
right up to the carotid arteries of his shirt collar.

Chaúque's barbers
left behind towels of dry leaves
with the appropriate purple stains.

---

* *SA Eng*, maize.

They Went There [44]

Grandma,
you don't need to go the hospital
tomorrow.

Yesterday they went there
they fired many-many shots
they broke everything, everything
they killed patients
they mutilated the male nurse
they raped the midwife.

The privileged patients
had to carry stuff on their heads
flour, sugar and rice
from the cooperative farm
. . .
They went.

Notes

The Pores of the Plague. The sense that the mass of people would sooner or later rise up is also present in this enigmatic poem, written at the time when censorship was particularly active (the book where the poem was published in came out only in 1974). We are presented with the image of the colonialist fat cat—fattened with all the blood it has drunk—who hears the chirping noise of millions of emerging rats. These are like 'the million pores' of the 'plague' which is about to overwhelm the country. It is quite probable that Craveirinha intended 'plague' to be a pun on 'Black Plague' (the pun exists also in Portuguese), since it is precisely 'blacks' who will rise up to reclaim their country.

Oh! Carmen de Diego. José Craveirinha is probably the Mozambican interpreter who does the most to go beyond the geographical space of Mozambique. This poem dates from the 1950s. It is a love poem to a real-life woman who was living in Lourenço Marques (now Maputo) at the time; it is also the evocation of her suffering, and in particular her rape in a barn, during the Spanish Civil War. From the starting point of this event the poem becomes a generalized evocation of the Spanish Civil War. It traverses various places, from north to south, from Catalonia to Andalusia, and each place name (Barcelona, Córdoba, Guadarrama, Guernica, Madrid, Malaga, San Sebastian) becomes a signpost to the immensity of the destruction and terror. In doing so, the poem becomes also an invocation to the 'martyred people of Spain', and the style, as if honouring their dead and their valour, becomes curiously evocative of that most famous of Spanish poets, Federico García Lorca, also one of the martyred, and one of the features of whose poetry was the surprising, turnabout metaphor. The original, written in a mixture of Spanish and Portuguese, attests to this attempt to bridge the boundaries, to reach out, ecumenically, in a gesture of compassion. (My concession to this was to translate all the Spanish place names and the names of Spanish folk dances, written in Portuguese in the original, back into Spanish.) The declamatory style might be alien to a reader accustomed to the civility of English verse where there are hardly ever any great shouts, but the sincerity of the love and rage should be obvious.

Maria Sende. The rise of African nationalism in colonial Mozambique was propelled and forced into the open, not only because African culture was neglected or marginalized but also because the African people of

Mozambique were oppressed. Mozambicans were often 'recruited' to work on the sisal and cotton plantations, others were 'recruited' to work on the Rand mines in South Africa. Colonial Mozambique was also a police state with its entire apparatus of secret police, censorship, arbitrary arrests. Despite all this, Mozambican nationalism—at least at this earlier stage—was quite inclusive. It bespoke a vision of a pluri-racial society, one where every colour and creed had its space. This poem even speaks of a type of cultural miscegenation, the dream of a country that is black and white and also 'raceless'. Racial colour is obliterated in the spiral of a common Mozambican identity.

Wax-Shine. This prison poem refers to both the real prison cell where José Craveirinha was incarcerated, and the metaphorical prison that the country had been transformed into. The growing climate of fear in the country—or perhaps in Lourenço Marques, the capital city—is compared to a shoeshine-boy who is making shoes shinier and shinier: that wax-shine is fear. It is in the context of fear that the reference to the hyena should be understood. A relatively common animal in Mozambique and a persistent figure of contempt in popular lore, the word carries with it powerful associations for Mozambican readers (more so because Craveirinha uses the Mozambican term *quizumba* rather than the standard Portuguese *hiena*). Essentially a cowardly animal, the carrion-eating hyena represents all that is gross and vile in the police state.

Our City. The poem describes life in Lourenço Marques in the early 1970s. The last three lines of the poem have been frequently quoted, even though the poem has never been included in any of Craveirinha's collections. The image is of a dirty and forsaken black boy. What is the price of the cupful of peanuts he is selling? Dirt cheap, the answer seems to be.

Canticle of the Blue Bird in Sharpeville. This is one of many poems inspired by events which occurred in South Africa. The Sharpeville Massacre took place on the 21st of March 1960 when 69 Africans protesting against the pass laws were shot in the back by the apartheid police. This poem can be read as an act of embrace to South Africa and the struggle of its martyred majority. It does not pretend to speak on behalf of South Africans, but instead uses the Mozambican experience of oppression as a basis from which to understand political repression and racial segregation in South Africa. The poem catalogues the kinds of oppression which existed in Mozambique—labourers forcibly recruited to work on farms and plantations, the servants in cotton uniforms, the meagre rations. This was the Mozambican equivalent of oppression in South Africa; it was not the same as what was happening in South Africa but sufficiently *like* it. The struggle for liberation in these countries is thus seen by the poet as a common struggle. The poem talks about the "the seeds of the Ronga" and "the wild flowers on the hills of the Zulus": the Ronga and the Zulus (who live on the adjoining sides of the border) are connected by ties of language and by similar ancestral traditions, and also, the poem would add, by a similar experience of oppression and a similar desire to resist. Because the intensity of this desire draws its substance from Africa—or, more metaphorically, from the African sky which is replete with ancient sorceries—their own resistance is likely to be bold and intense. The song of the blue bird singing in the arms of a baobab tree heralds the 'terrible voluptuousness' of the flight or ascent of the oppressed majority as they rise up.

The Tasty Tanjarines of Inhambane. This was Craveirinha's first great post-revolutionary poem. The poem criticizes those writers (the 'makers of poesy') who, in their reluctance to criticize some of the inequalities and injustices in the new society for fear of being deemed unpatriotic or 'enemies of the Revolution', turned poetry into a denial of reality. Craveirinha, who had courageously attacked the injustices of colonialism, remained firmly coherent in his position. There were inequalities, and these needed to be spoken out. The tone of his poem lacks the incisive hostility of his anti-colonial poems, but the note of reproof is still there. The poem is also an attack on nepotism, incompetence, and on the hypocrisy of blaming colonialism for all societal ills; it also criticizes those who nostalgically look back to the colonial days as a time of plenty. One final note about the word 'tanjarine': the word is as it should be: in Portuguese the correct spelling is *tangerina* (the word is etymologically derived from *Tânger*, Tangiers), yet Craveirinha writes it as *tanjarina*. He is talking about something specifically Mozambican. In his typed version of this poem, Craveirinha inserts a special note, asking 'the *xicuembo* [other-worldly spirit] of the proofreaders not to correct the word', for that would be 'to correct incorrectly'.

Land of Canaan. The poem is a critique of the State of Israel's aggression against Palestinians. For the poet, the actions of the State of Israel are, ironically, reminiscent of Nazi tyranny. The poem might appear, at first reading, to be somewhat anti-Semitic, but for Craveirinha it is the danger of forgetting the Holocaust and the Jews' own persecution under the Nazis that is at source of this baseness. Modern-day Jews—and most Israelis are Jews—have psychologically identified with their own persecutors: they have become like them and hate themselves for it. The image of the Israeli pilot flying 'towards Eichmann' represents the self-loathing of a nation that has forgotten the sad and tragic history of so many of its own people.

Why? and **Necklaces.** The word 'necklaces' refers to the rubber tyres which were placed around the necks of collaborators, doused with petrol, and set alight. This particularly gruesome kind of death became very common in the turbulent South African townships of the 1980s, often administered by what were then called 'people's courts'. What these poems react to, though, was Winnie Mandela's open support for this sort of punishment being meted out on those who, traitorously, collaborated with the apartheid regime. These are the actual words Mrs Mandela used at rally in Soweto in April 1986: "We have no arms. But we have stones. We have our boxes of matches. We have our bottles. [. . .] With our necklaces, we will liberate this country!" The thrust of the poem "Necklaces", which is *dedicated to* Winnie Mandela, is that these so-called 'collaborators' were her brothers, and that she had got the enemy wrong. Winnie Mandela had appropriated for herself the role of an omnipotent being, one that made Jupiter in Olympus or even the mighty Afrikaners look less like gods, for unlike her they did not devour their own. "Why?" (the title in the original is in English) addresses Winnie Mandela directly. The poem describes how a necklaced person dies; it is like an 'after-shave' that has gone horribly wrong, and melts everything into tar. He suggests that the horror of this image should make her—as it makes him, and would no doubt make her jailed husband—averse to these cheap fireworks displays. The poem ends with the words "why?". It is as if we are in the face of something as uncomprehending as the Israeli pilot whose heart is as black as the Nazi nightmare.

Communiqué from Cuíto Cuanavale. This poem is dedicated to five of the most important Angolan writers and poets (Jacinto, Luandino, Pepetela, David Mestre and Mitó). Cuíto Cuanavale refers to the South African attack on the Angolan town with that name during the apartheid era, ending in the defeat of the South Africans; this was the most significant turning point in the war in Angola, and the beginning of the end of apartheid. But this is also a poem about South Africa under PW Botha. It offers up a mirror to South Africa, a refracted mirror, one where it can see its own image reflected back. It may be argued that this image is obscured by the anger with which it is portrayed. The image of crazy and racist demagogues out on a spree is certainly present in the poem. Their bombs are "cancerous eggs", their planes "vile praetorian Impalas", a pun on the adjective for Pretoria. But it is more than a poem of condemnation and outrage. The image is also that of a nation being devoured by the violence it begets; there is a sense of pity for the wastefulness of it all, like the "ideological suicide" of the Afrikaner boy trapped in the 'laughter' of the flames of the plane shot down by the Angolans.

De Profundis; Burnt Down Village; Gluttony; Barber's Shop; and They Went There. These poems, bar one, are taken from a collection entitled *Babalaze das Hienas*, which means 'The Hangover of the Hyenas'. South African readers will probably recognize the similarity of the word *babalaze* to *babalaas*, the word for hangover, originally Afrikaans, but used also by English-speaking South Africans. The 'hyenas' refers to the armed bandits. See the explanatory notes on Luís Carlos Patraquim's "Carnivorous Elegy" for a discussion on armed banditry.

GLÓRIA de SANT'ANNA (1925 - 2009)

- *Distância* (1951)
- *Música Ausente* (1954)
- *Livro de Água* (1961)
- *Poemas do Tempo Agreste* (1964)
- *Um Denso Azul Silêncio* (1965)
- *Desde que o Mundo* (1972)
- *Amaranto* (1988) — collected poems, 1951-1983
- *Não Eram Aves Marinhas* (1988)
- *Solamplo* (2000) — collected poems, 1961-1975
- *Algures no Tempo* (2005)
- *Trinado para a Noite que Avança* (2009)

Widely regarded by some as representing one of the highest achievements in Mozambican lyricism, Glória de Sant'Anna's work is ignored—*delenda gloria*—by many others. Six of her poetry collections were published *in* Mozambique. The silence which surrounds this poet seems to reflect more on the ideological and racial preconceptions of the Mozambican canon-makers (many of whom are not Mozambican) than on considerations of her unique achievement, which is not generally denied. The Portuguese likewise tend to treat her work with a similar silence, a refusal to engage in, rather a dismissal of, her work; the suggestion is that she cannot be placed within that tradition either. The poet is however held in high esteem by the Mozambican poets themselves and the lineage initiated by Glória de Sant'Anna is today one of the dominant traditions in Mozambican lyricism. A school teacher for most of her life, she worked in Porto Amélia (now called Pemba) and Vila Pery (now Chimoio). Glória de Sant'Anna, retired for many years, lived in Óvar, Portugal.

Stained Glass [45]
—1951

You have me here, kneeling,
my hands listless,
the eyelids hung in silence.

The only thing that remains
within the sweet and vacant shadow
is an ancient and exacting problem.

And a shaft from the moon
breaks through my heart of glass.

Drawing on the Sand [46]
—1961

On the smooth pale water.
The whelk arrayed in nacre.

(What slow, broken sentence,
what faint and estranged word?)

On the smooth white sand.
The left-over shell of a whelk.

(What broken smile,
or what shattered destiny?)

Whelk of nacre, and the rose,
the colour also of dead pearls,
and the sun, the light, the shadow
and the moon and the dead hour;

of calm and translucent water,
sea spume and thick sea wrack,
and also recollections and worries,
whelk of memory and tenderness.

Left behind
on the smooth pale water.

Cast
on the warm white sand.

(Sing your secret message
in my ear.)

Condition [47]
—1961

Walking over the clear, see-through whelks
and the slow-moving seaweed,
the black woman unweaves her quiet steps.

Looking for shell-fish
next to the wet and immersed rocks,
the black woman sighs with tiredness.

(Arising from the depths of time,
the black woman bends over the restless water
and over her round basket
of woven straw.
Deep within the afternoon,
the black woman bends over the closed
line of sky,
and the gesture is both ancestral
and tired.)

Walking over the clear, see-through whelks
and the white seashells,
the black woman is silent
and the path swerves.

Stars were born from within the dark waters.

Walking black woman,
what do they say, the stars that guide your footsteps?

Marine [48]
—1961

The fish glides in the calm water
inside the clear and translucent water.
Guided by its instinct.
Hunger has him killed.

The fish slips into the easy snare.
(Its back is of silver, the mandible of corals.)

It slips into the intense mortal clarity
above its head among the sharp seaweed.
Already imprisoned, already dead.
But still of silver.

The fish stirs within the smooth snare.
(I confound the cold pupils with glass.)

For the fisherman is coming
and his footsteps
are those of strength and sun
and hope and water.

And under the quiet
mortal clarity
The fish is of silver,
of blood and salt.

Rough Poem [49]
—1964

I don't know why you look for those long words
to describe the short-lived things which frighten us.

I don't know why you weave huge webs
to describe the uncertainties which enfold us.

I don't know why you persist. I don't know why you persist
in imprisoning my steps within these boundaries.

Nocturne [50]
—1965

The night drowses into invisible and drawn-out sleep
inside the slender fingers of the quiet trees

alongside the dainty birds with vacant eyes
in the clear dawn that is still to emerge.

The full and dispersed blue silence is felt again
and a quivering breeze that doesn't even exist pretends to stir

(and it would draw the contours of the dull, faint walls
without touching the secret and unknown innermost of the stone).

Everything is inside the fixed mark of its own boundary.

Only the sea rises and restlessly reflects
the useless and tired vigil of the stars.

Eighth Poem [51]
—1961-1971

ah, Our Lord of Nangololo,[*]
covered in the darkness
of your slashed face
as if everything wasn't already
(crown, wood, carnations)
the announced end.

ah, Christ of Nangololo,
crucified all over again.

---

[*] Nangololo (sometimes also spelt Ngangololo) refers to a mission station where, in 1964, a group of FRELIMO dissidents murdered a Dutch priest.

Sixth Poem [52]
—1961-1971

(*the exodus of the Makonde**)

Where are they, these people
who stepped out from the mists of time?

They had dark huts
grouped in circles
the colour of which merged
with the ancient trunks
of the tall moist trees
that were part of the horizon.

Their faces were marked
with the symmetrical scars
that tied them to an unknown custom
where women carried in their lips
a wound healed by a gem
the colour almost of the moonlight.

And they had long assegais
of a pure and shining iron
yielded to them in the set-out
pre-historic moment
and they had rough-textured shields
made from pale skins dappled
by large blots of sunlight.

Where do they go, these people
who stepped out from the depths of time?

---

* The Makonde, a tribe from Northern Mozambique famous for its expressionistic
ebony sculptures. Living, as they were, in one of the war-zones, during the war many
of the Makonde fled across the border to Tanzania.

They were swift like the wind
and their triangular teeth
were quick on their faces . . .
But in their eyes there was
the indwelling of the certainty
of the light, the colour and weight
which was born from their fingers
and grew into the lean shapes
carved out of ebony.

(each shape grew from their black hands
as if it had sprouted unto the brightness
from under the thin layer of skin
and carried with it the rustic traces,
and in their faces
and in their water-soaked pupils
there was the same secret time for loving)

Today the weighty and mysterious ebony
stands at the centre of all absence,
it is full of those unrecognizable shapes
that move in the same manner as those in our memory
even though they belong to a different order
and another time.

But the huts (some of them)
wait, even though they look sombre,
still carrying the lukewarm memory
of the ash from the home
scattered by the wind over the fallen grass
or kept afloat on the water
as though a short-lived flower bud.

And the roots
having absorbed the flesh from the dead
lift the strong sap to the highest branch
and through the open petals,
they cast into the sky
the glowing hope of a return.

Ever Since the World [53]
—1972

The world is welling up
with blood
and a thousand eyes look at us from the depths

Every bud that bursts is filled with blood
filled with blood
and in the centre there is a hard eye

The faces, the faces, the silent faces
that were of flesh and are of earth
and the teeth, the teeth, the teeth scattered
in between   inside   in the middle of stones

And the ears, ears, lying and listening
listening   waiting   listening   waiting
for the steps and the heart-beat   the voices   the smoke
and the wind and the rain and the turning of the world

And eating the earth's hunger for blood

in between bones and skin
in between bones and skin

weevils, weevils, weevils, weevils
sharing everything

Poem of the Sea [54]
—1972

In the deep a fisherman is dead.
And his foot is propped by a coral.
The *m'cota*[*] was dissolved and he is naked
—naked in the freedom of the sea.

Quick and slender seaweed grazes
past his face, still silent and intact,
and through the open eyes
there are liquid green images.

His arms are raised. And the hands,
like pale unfolded flowers,
glide quietly through
the measure of the water.

Those on the surface who search for him
don't know how perfect and complete he is,
tied by his last coral
to the memory of all he loved.

And so, all words,
all calls, shouts, tears
are dispersed into the shadow of the wind
and into the secret blue of the water.

[Translated with Glória de Sant'Anna]

---

[*] A type of loin-cloth, sometimes made of animal hide, and tied by a string.

Sea [55]
—1972

Why is it always the sea?
Because it is concrete,
filled with the dead and true

As we leave the pale wake
astern of the moving ship
everything becomes of sea-human origin

Even I, you,
we walk with this warm water,
in this transposed water

Why is it always the sea:
it's that
—the dead, the seaweed, the tides, the living.

(And also the form,
the colour, the weave,
suggested by the brightness of time of day.)

Second Poem on Solitude [56]
—1972

I shall be as secret
as the texture of the water

and so light

and so beyond myself that I allow the whole landscape
to flow through me

and so, too, the careless sin
of gesture, presence or word

and when your hand detains me
you shall see that I am not there:

I shall be water

"but on the other hand our joy . . ." [57]
—1970-1974

but on the other hand our joy could also burst open
in a lightning flash in full view
over what we call sky

and unbelievable birds would fly
over what we call sky
and colts with the long manes of the wind
would beat their hooves unshackled by iron
in a gallop over what resembled a field

and someone could claim that he had seen us
by the uncontrolled strength of our joy.

"in Knossos there was a man . . ." [58]
—1978-1983

in Knossos there was a man
who was clothed in salt

he drank wine at lunch-time
and honeyed water for dinner

he sang verses of rain
and twined moonbeams into flowers

yesterday they killed that man
with knives that had still to be sharpened

and this blood which covers me
tastes of wine and it tastes of salt
honeyed water and the rain
and the flowers from the jacaranda

"my dry eyes . . ." [59]
—1978-1983

my dry eyes drift
on the clear blue of the sea
—two transparent barges
in mourning

in the still atmosphere
the shore has no contours
—two heartsore castaways
that were almost drowned

the morning bursts open
with vain splendour
ay   where do I go
with my lost eyes

ay   my eyes   two barges
ay   my drowned dreams
—ay   so much love
which lost its way in the water

Mill

the wood sounds patient and alive
in each upright and ancient movement
that I follow

the firm fingers grasping the mortar
are covered with dust particles

it is this vast melody from the seesawing
rhythm   calm   so very calm
from all those thousands of years

—   and I know I have stepped
     into the time of water and fire
     of myths and forebodings
     and that a weightless halo from the ashes
     rests lightly over my hair —

The Castle Windmill

the creaking of the wood is patient and alive
in each of the ancient steps
that I climb up

I feel the loose particles of dust
on the fingers that quickly touch the handrail

and the vast structure of the windmill
seesaws calmly   so very calmly
in all its many centuries

— and I imagine that I have stepped
    inside the warm time
    of the loom   of the woollen cloths
    where a pure halo from the wheat
    rests softly over my hair —

The Old Fisherman [62]
—1989

fisherman from the wide sea
with your shoes of seaweed
tell me what you bring in the boat
from where you raise your face

your face stained
by the salt of hours spent crying,
give me your fish hauled
from well into the depths of the ocean

—in this water there's no fish—

fisherman, give me only one fish
not a grouper or even a giant trevally
only a small silver fish

—in this water there are no fish
they all went to search for god
on the sides of Zanzibar—

Poem [63]
—c. 1992

go and cast my words
into the overflow of loose sand
between the baobabs and the high tide

they will merge
with the tender edge of the seaweed
all of them diluting in the water
all of them acquiring that essence
of having been reclaimed

because this poem is for the sea

Erotica [64]
—2004

On the publication of Ana Mafalda's[*] fifth book.

the camels broke loose

the *kafila*[†]
hurtles over the sand
the mouths of the camels opened wide

the load topples over

the air's astir with
              cardamom   benzoin
              pepper and camphor

sheer *kabayas*[‡]
swirl
over the gold and the saris

              dispersed cinnamon
              za'faran[§]

close to the enlaced bodies caressing each other

the camels broke loose

and poetry's everything
that dissolves in the air
in lost aromas

---

[*] Ana Mafalda Leite's fifth collection, *Passaporte do Coração* (2002). See, for example, "An Island Sails in My Soul."

[†] *Swahili*, caravan.

[‡] *Malay*, sarongs.

[§] *Arabic*, saffron.

aroma   spices   fragrances
doleful hands

and the bodies enlaced on the sand

the silk veils
            kabayas

and the Arabs
the Arabs and the whelks
have been joined

to the doleful bodies on the sand

the camels broke loose

the *kafila* hurtles
            the mouths of the camels opened wide
foaming

and poetry
is those bodies on the sand that have been satiated

spices
            aromas
ginger and cinnamon

over the bodies made naked by the sand

Setting Music for the *Rebab* [65*]
—2005

To José Craveirinha

The warm sand
swallows your footsteps

and your measured
words
are present in your wide eyes

which linger in the sorrows
of the hard times
of other ages past

Arabic brother
for you are also of the Algarve

here I sing
your bronze tone
and your wisdom

living statue under the warm sun
of the warm sand of Mafalala

---

* The *rebab* (*arrabil* in Portuguese) is an ancient Arabic or Persian stringed
instrument; it may be the ancestor of our violin and fiddle.

Notes

Stained Glass. The term 'stained glass' (*vitral*) clearly refers to a stained glass window in church, probably with the depiction of an event from the life of Christ. This early church poem introduces us to a theme later taken up in "Eighth Poem".

Rough Poem. This 'rough poem' is taken from a collection whose title literally means 'Poems from a Rough Time'. The balanced cadences, the measured pace, the careful weighing of each word, the intimate concerns, which so often speak of conjugal love, contrast markedly with the sort of poetry that was being written at about the same time, which so often has the raw edge of the immediacy of an active involvement in history.

Eighth Poem. The eighth poem in a cycle of poems on the Colonial War; although written between 1964 and 1971, these were published only in 1988, when Glória de Sant'Anna's collected poems came out. The poem centres on the image of the crucified Christ in the church at Nangololo— Our Lord of Nangololo—the Christ who had died for the sins of humankind. But for Glória de Sant'Anna, as for any orthodox Christian, the Incarnation is a continual process; the community of believers is also the 'body of Christ'. That 'body of Christ' is being crucified all over again. The crown of thorns, the wood of the cross of the carnations in the mission church at Nangololo do not announce the end of the suffering of the people of God.

Ever Since the World. The poem suggests that the violence and the blood were things that sprung from a much deeper, more frightening centre, some sort of unconscious universal well. The poem is also the title of a collection published in Mozambique in 1972; her two numbered war poems, which speak more directly about the war situation, were written at about the same time. There may have been a link between the allegorical portrayal of violence and censorship, which would not have permitted such an open speaking out about the war.

Poem of the Sea; Sea & Second Poem on Solitude. There is something singularly unhistorical about the way Glória de Sant'Anna's poetry is deployed to speak of the Indian Ocean; this was not the sort of poetry Craveirinha was writing in the 1970s. But the maritime motifs point to much more than a mere sea-obsession: the texture of the water suggests a seamless poetic texture, one where limpidity is at the very heart of the poem. It is no coincidence that this 'maritime poetry' is also one of exemplary lucidity. But these encounters with liquid chambers of the ocean, 'the secret blue of the water', 'the secret texture of the water', suggest other lessons: water as a revelation of life and the essence of life.

"in Knossos there was a man . . ." & **"my dry eyes . . ."** These poems of exile speak of loss at a much more universal level. The first poem makes a conscious allusion to the pre-Christian, Hellenic conception of man as being consubstantial with nature, with the elements and the fruits of nature. The murder of such a man not only creates a violent rupture with the previous order of nature, it also suggests, the loss of all innocence. Yet the reminders of the previous world are never obliterated; they remain, as the elemental signs of the loss: the blood that covers the murdered man has the same taste as all those things from his previous life: wine, salt, honeyed water, rain, and jacaranda blossoms. The second poem uses images of the sea to suggest the permanent loss of exile and the sadness that comes with it: the eyes that gaze on the distance are as liquid as the water itself.

Mill & **The Castle Windmill**. These two poems are very similar, but they were written in different periods and at different places: "Mill" was written in Mozambique in the 1950s; "The Castle Windmill" was composed during a trip to Malmö in Sweden in the late 1970s.

The Old Fisherman. Removed from the day-to-day Mozambican reality by her exile, this poem from 1989 speaks of maintained interest in Mozambique. This is a dolorous poem about the poverty of a sea that no longer yields fish; instead of blaming this dearth on over-fishing the poet suggests, more kindly, that all the fish have gone 'to search for god' in the mythical seas around Zanzibar.

Setting Music for the *Rebab*. The poem is Glória de Sant'Anna's tribute to José Craveirinha, who died in 2003. The poet's father was from the Algarve, as was Craveirinha's father. The Algarve was the last part of Portugal to be taken from the Arabs (or, more specifically, the Moors), and a place where the vestiges of Arab civilization are most evident. The word Algarve is itself derived from the Arabic (*El Gharb*, the West). It is appropriate that the poet should describe her song as a musical setting for the *rebab*, an Arabic musical instrument which still exists in the Algarve.

NOÉMIA de SOUSA (1926 - 2002)

- *Sangue Negro* (2001)

Rightly considered one of Africa's greatest women poets, Noémia de Sousa published her first poems in 1948, when she was 22. Her almost total poetic output was written in the following three years, and she did not write again until 1988, when she composed a poem on the death of Samora Machel. In 1951 she went on holiday to Lisbon and stayed. Later she moved to Paris. She returned to Portugal after the 1974 Revolution. She did not—as it has been claimed—stop writing because she married a Portuguese man. (The poet was married to a Mozambican who, like her, happened to have been a Portuguese national because he had been born in a Portuguese colony.) According to Noémia de Sousa she never really stopped writing; she was a journalist and the writing she produced after she moved to Europe was of a different nature. Her powerful poetic work, which influenced a whole generation of writers and poets, remained uncollected for almost fifty years: *Sangue Negro* came out in 2001. She died in Lisbon.

Boss [66]
—1949

Boss, boss, oh my boss!
Why d'you always beat me up,
with no pity at all,
with your hard and hostile eyes,
with your words that are as cutting as arrows,
with that look of sharp disdain,
and sometimes
with a humiliating clout from your own hand,
even though everything I do
is by nature submissive?

Oh, why boss? Tell me just this:
what harm did I do you?
(Was it because I was born with this skin colour?)

Boss, I don't know anything . . . You can see
they didn't teach me anything,
only how to hate and obey . . .
Only how to hate and obey, yes!
But when I speak, boss, you laugh
and that man, Boss Manuel Soares[*]
from the Rádio Clube[†] also laughs . . .
I don't understand your Portuguese,
boss, my Landim[‡] I know well,
and it's a language as beautiful
and as dignified as yours, boss . . .
In my heart there is none other, better,
more mild and gentle as that one!

---

[*] Manuel Soares was a radio announcer in the 1940s notorious for imitating 'black' accents.
[†] Rádio Clube de Moçambique was the biggest privately-owned radio station in Mozambique; it began broadcasting in 1933.
[‡] 'Landim' was the name the Portuguese gave to xi-Ronga, the language of the Ronga tribe from Southern Mozambique.

So why d'you laugh at me?

Ah, boss, I built
this mulatto land of Mozambique
with the strength of my love,
with the sweat of my sacrifice,
with the flesh of my will!
I built it, boss,
stone by stone, house by house,
tree by tree, city by city,
with happiness and pain!
I built it!

And if your mind doesn't want to believe me,
ask your house who it was who made each of its bricks,
who got up onto the scaffolding,
who cleans it now and makes it so pretty,
who scours and sweeps and polishes . . .?
Ask, also, the acacias, red and sensual
as the lips of your little girls,
who planted and watered them
and later pruned them . . .?
Ask all those wide city streets,
symmetrical and dark and glittering,
who was it who tarred them,
even despite the hell of a summer sun . . .?
Ask also who sweeps them,
early in the morning, when the dew covers everything . . .
Ask who dies at the docks
everyday—every single day!—
only to be resurrected by a song . . .?
And who's the slave on the sisal and cotton plantations
throughout this Mozambique . . .?
Sisal and cotton which will be set aside for you
and not for me, my boss . . .

And the sweat is mine,
the pain is mine,
the sacrifice is mine,
the land is my own,

and the sky is too!

And you hit me, my boss!
You hit me . . .
And the blood spreads, and it will become sea . . .
Boss, beware,
because a sea of blood can drown
everything . . . even you, my boss!
Even you . . .

Samba [67]
—1949

In the hollow of the ballroom dance-hall
filled with the fictitious lights of civilization
and the false laughter
and the hand-painted dresses
and the frizzy hair
which civilization has de-frizzed,
the sudden sounding of the jazz percussion
soared like a cry of freedom,
like a spear that tore away
the cellophane wrapped around the contrived poses.

Then
came the subdued sound of the guitar
joining in with the warm pulsating of Mother Africa
on those nights of a thousand anxieties,
then came the saxophone
and the piano
and the rattles hissing the rhythms of the cow-hide drum,
and the whole dance-hall threw away the duplicity of the hired poses
and it reeled.
It reeled!

And the fictitious lights ceased to exist.
And who said the soft warm light shed on the floor
wasn't the very moonlight of the *shigombelas**?
And who said the palms and the coconut trees,
the cashews,
the marula trees,
hadn't come to circle the cow-hide drums
with their swinging shadows?
Ah! In that familiar landscape

---

* A Mozambican dance usually performed at weddings and danced by separate lines
of men and women.

the laughing smiles became as pure as the white of the manioc,
the trill of the dance brought back the ancient fever
of the far-distant cow-hide drums,
and the glittering dresses of civilization were gone
and the bodies rose, victorious,
gleaming in the samba,[†]
dancing, dancing . . .

The fraternal rhythms of the samba
bringing out all the voodoo sorceries,
the hollow strokes of the marimbas shrieking out
the broken pieces of a slave's lament,
oh, the fraternal rhythms of Bahia's warm samba!
Setting the explosive blood of the mulattos on fire,
making the prudish high-heels of the women quiver,
injecting the dancing legs of the blacks
with sorceries and madness . . .
The fraternal rhythms of the samba,
a heritage of Africa the slaves took with them
in the sunless wombs of the slave ships
and set free, even though they were manacled
and filled with longing,
into the warm nights of the Southern Cross!
Oh, the fraternal rhythms of the samba,
awakening malarial fevers in my people,
long-dulled by a prescription of European quinine . . .
the African rhythms of Bahia's samba,
with the rattles hissing out the beats of fever
—what's the Bahiana got, what's it?—
and the guitars weaving the sorceries of the *xicuembos*
and the kettle-drums soaring with a languid sound. . .

Oh, the fraternal rhythms of the samba!
Awakening my people who have fallen asleep
under the shade of the baobabs,
telling us in its language of many rhythms

[†] The samba is a fast and lively Brazilian dance with syncopated rhythms; it originated in the Brazilian state of Bahia where most of the population is of African/slave origin.

121

that the shackles of the slave ships never died, no,
they just changed name,
but still continue,
oh, the fraternal rhythms of the samba continue still!

Poem for Rui de Noronha [68]
—1949

(*on the anniversary of his death*)

The tracks slashed open by the cutlass
in the wild bushveld of our native land
are moving in a direction which is new to us,
single and unalterable . . .
A path of sharp points—oh yes—of thorns,
but still a path for our wounded feet to walk on,
and take us there, O Poet. . .
Before the new horizons which open themselves like a gift to us
our souls which have been resigned now learn to desire
both with strength and in rage,
and they rise up, warrior-like,
ready to face the hard struggle,
And our mouths become a single closed line
in that final 'No' of a vigilant sentry.

Rui de Noronha,
in this new Africa restored to its strengths and certainties
you come to me, all tormented and solitary
even though you are in the midst of passionate affairs
and the drunkenness of Christmas-time,
still gazing into the deep crevices of your inner world,
those green precipices of boredom and dissatisfaction . . .
You come to me, O Poet, bleeding with your loves,
your inhuman loves,
with suicidal despair and the vaingloriousness of a Brahmin
swallowing up your whole human life.

But even though you come to me, O Poet,
all banished and tragic,
I shelter you within my warm kanga of understanding
and I lull you with the music of that sweetest song
I learnt from my black grandmother . . .

Sleep, O Poet,
sleep that slumber you desired so much,
rest now, after all those fictitious tragedies which alone were yours,
and don't pay any attention to the song . . .
Allow its tenderness to heal the wounds
but don't pay any attention to it, no!
It may awaken the *xipócuê*[*] of remorse,
for the song brings with it the most powerful sorceries
of the *ngomas*[†] of Maputo,[‡]
the land of my black grandmother.
And perhaps it will ask you very gently:
ah, what did you do for me, O Poet,
always so deaf and blind and insensitive,
what did you do for Africa?
—Didn't it pass you by and yet you did not see it?
—didn't it raise itself and yet you did not sense it?
—didn't it cry out and yet you did not hear it?
and the remorse, O Poet, would be so painful,
like an army of chigoes assailing your whole body.

Sleep, sleep, oh Rui de Noronha,
my brother,
carry on sleeping,
imprisoned in the walled-up hut of your inner world.
Don't heed to the song—it's too late now . . .

But as for that dying and weak torchlight
which those hands of yours, almost translucent,
barely tolerated holding,
give it to us, for we'll take it!
We will give it life with the resin of our agonies,
we will raise that flame with all our lit fires,
and this life-flame
will be the fire of our self-renewing hope!

---

[*] *Xi-Ronga*, a soul from the other world.
[†] A *ngoma* is a cow-hide drum, normally used during a dance, the *anginya*,
performed only by women.
[‡] The area in the south of Mozambique, adjoining the South African province of
Kwazulu-Natal; not to be confused with the city now known as Maputo.

And then, oh then,
when our hands, strong and bronzed,
have raised it like a banner to the heights of life
may that blood-coloured flame of unblemished brightness
be our guide and inspiration
and spur on the rebellion within our swollen veins.

Like a comet
crossing the night of our crushed breasts.

Poem of a Distant Childhood [69]
—1950

When I was born in the large house by the shore of the sea,
it was midday and the sun shone brightly over the Indian Ocean.
Seagulls hovered in the air, white, drunk with the blue.
The boats of the Indian fisherman still had to return,
hauling their burdened nets.
On the bridge, the shouts of the blacks on the boats
calling out to the mamas drowsy with the heat,
with bundles on their heads
and snotty children on their backs,
soared like a faraway sound,
faraway as it hung in the haze of silence.
While on the scorching steps,
dozed off Mufasini the beggar,
surrounded by flies.

When I was born . . .
—I know the air was calm, at rest (so they told me)
and the sun shone brightly over the sea.
In the middle of all that stillness
I was hurled into the world,
already carrying my stigma.
And I cried and howled—I don't even know why.
Ah, but as life went on
my tears dried under the light of a flame of indignation.
And the sun never shone as brightly as it did
on the those first days of my existence,
even though the bright and endless
seascape of my childhood,
constantly calm like a swamp,
has been the guide to all my adolescent steps,
as well as to my stigma.
But there is more, more still:
there were the varied companions of my childhood.

My companions of the fishing trips under the bridge
where we used a pin as a fish-hook
and a cotton thread as a fishing line,
my tattered companions with bellies as round as pumpkins,
companions in the games and races
through the fields and beaches of Catembe,
companions united by the marvel
of discovering a nest of warblers,
of making a bird-trap made of gum,
of hunting for tree agamas* and humming birds,
of chasing after butterflies under a hot Summer sun. . .
—Unforgettable images of my boyish childhood,
free and happy:
children who were black and mulatto, Indian and white,
sons of the maid, of the baker,
of the black boatman, of the carpenter,
coming both from the squalor of Guachene
and the wooden houses of the fishermen,
the district commissioner's spoilt children,
the bright-spark sons of the coast-guards
—brothers in an adventure that was always new,
from the raids on the cashews in the plots
to the secret taste of the sweetest of monkey-oranges,†
companions in the disquieting sensation
of the mystery of the 'Island of Lost Ships'
—where no cry was left without an echo.

Ah, my companions squatting in the enthralling
and awesome circle of the *Karingana wa Karingana*‡
in the stories retold by the old man from Maputo
during the twilights of dark and terrifying thunderstorms
(the wind howling against the zinc roof,
the sea threatening to knock down
the wooden steps of the veranda

---

* The Southern tree agama (*agama atricollis*), the blue-headed lizard.
† Also known as *maçala*, the monkey-orange is an edible wild fruit, similar to the orange; its scientific name is *strychnos spinosa*.
‡ The ritual formula of invocation used to introduce a tale, similar to the English 'Once upon a time'.

and the casuarinas wailing, wailing,
oh wailing without consolation,
awakening strange and inexplicable fears
in our souls filled with visions of toothless bogeymen
and of the kings of Massinga
who turned into boa constrictors . . .)
Ah, my companions planted in me the seed of dissatisfaction
that grows more dissatisfied day by day.
They filled my childhood with the sun that shone
on the day I was born.
With their luminous, unthinking comradeship,
their radiant joy,
their excited enthusiasm
at any paper kite that took flight
in a sky of a Technicolor blue,
with their unwritten and every-ready loyalty
they filled my boyish childhood
with unforgettable joys and adventures.

And if today the sun doesn't shine as brightly
as it did on that day
I was born in the large house
on the shore of the Indian Ocean
I will not allow myself to fall asleep in the darkness.
My companions proved to be sure guides
in the journey through the road of life.

They proved to me that 'fraternity'
is not merely a pretty word
written in black in the dictionary on the shelf:
They taught me that 'fraternity' is a beautiful sentiment
and that it can be achieved,
even when the skin colour and the world around us
are so different.

That is why I BELIEVE that one day
the sun will once again shine brightly,
calm over the Indian Ocean.
Seagulls will hover in the air,
white, drunk with the blue,

and the fishermen will sing once more
as they sail over the still waters.
And this poison which pain
injected into my blood stream
on the nights of the dance of the cow-hide drum
will cease, forever, to disturb me.
One day,
the sun will flood the whole of life
and it will be like a new childhood
spreading its rays to everyone . . .

Magaíça [70*]
—1950

The blue and golden morning
of the tourist brochures
overwhelmed the simpleton,
dizzy at the incomprehensible
hubbub of the whites at the station
and the tremulous puffing of the trains,
his eyes stared with astonishment,
his heart knotted by the anguish of the unknown,
his bundle of rags
carrying the enormous anxiety that was woven
with all his wished-for dreams.

And one day,
the train returned, chuffing, chuffing . . .
oh, indeed, he has returned!

And on the train was the migrant
in an overcoat, with a scarf, striped socks,
an alien being
ridiculously attired.

On your back you carry the suitcases
—where did you leave your bundle of dreams, migrant?—
all filled with the false glitter
of the leftovers of the false civilization
of the Rand compounds.
Stunned
the migrant lit the lamp
searching in his hand for the lost illusions,
his youth and health
which had been buried back there on the mines in Jo'burg. . .

---

* A Mozambican miner who has returned home after having worked in the
Witwatersrand gold mines in South Africa.

Youth and health,
the lost illusions
that on dazzling nights
will shine like stars
over the low neck of any lady
in any city.

The Woman who Laughs at Life and Death [71]
—1991

Out there beyond the swerve
the ancestral spirits await me

Soon, very soon,
I will take my place among my forebears

To the land I will leave the remnants of my useless body,
the corneous nails of all efforts,
this casing furrowed by the spider of time

Before I am called to speak with the voice of a *nyanga**
each day is a victory
I greet it with the irreverent laughter of my secret triumph

Oyo, oyo, life!

Out there beyond the swerve
the ancestral spirits await me

---

* *Shangaan*, a traditional healer *or* an ancestral spirit.

Notes

Samba. The poem is a critique of Western civilization and an affirmation of Africa's ancestral qualities. Western civilization as it had been imposed on Africa is seen in terms of falsity. The poet talks about the 'the duplicity of the hired poses' of those forced to act European. The adoption of a Western-type civilization implies the negation of what is African. One of the ways in which this is done is through the imposition of Western standards of beauty, such as the 'frizzy' hair which the pretty girls in the poem want to have straightened. The falsity of Western-imposed civilization is contrasted with the 'victorious' dancing of the Brazilian *samba*. The poem suggests a profound link between the mysterious rhythms of Africa and the history of slavery and oppression. It is also an ecumenical poem, one that links the struggles of Mozambicans with those of black Brazilians.

Poem for Rui de Noronha. The appearance of modern Mozambican poetry coincided with the rise of an African consciousness, the precursor of what we would call African nationalism. This characteristic is already evident, even if ambiguously, in the work of Rui de Noronha (1909-1943). The one poem by Noronha where we observe African nationalism at its incipient stage is his sonnet "Rise Up and Walk". The poem is a plea for Africa to rise up and become *like* Europe, that is to say, to join the modern world, the world of Progress and civilization. But the new poetry which appeared in the late 1940s (such as the two previous poems by Noémia de Sousa) presented a very different vision of 'Africa's progress': Africa, this poetry insisted, could only rise up if it became truly African, if it drew on its roots, its traditions, those impulses, often ancient in origin, which have been submerged under the weight of colonialism. For Noémia de Sousa, these ancient beliefs, 'sorceries' and traditions were the only ones capable of 'awakening malarial fevers' in a people long-accustomed to 'European quinine'. It is Rui de Noronha's belief in African progress, politically misguided, that Noémia de Sousa reacts to in her poem. She also criticizes the older poet for what she perceives as the tortured quality of his poetry. Yet she acknowledges him to be a precursor of modern Mozambican poetry/nationalism, the two being closely allied. Despite his faults he was the father, the older brother, the way-paver. He was the one who, in his oblique way, heralded that 'comet' of Mozambican liberation.

Poem of a Distant Childhood. This autobiographical poem is probably the most famous elegy to the 'fraternal' solidarity between the 'races'. The poet describes all the various adventures that the poet-narrator and her companions shared, from raiding the cashew trees, to hunting for lizards and listening to stories of terror being told by an old black man. It was precisely because the experience of solidarity was so real that it could be possible to create a future that was just and free of oppression and the pain of injustice. The three opening lines are probably among the most famous lines of verse in Mozambican literature.

Magaíça. A Mozambican who went to work on the Rand mines in South Africa—because of the lure of money and trinkets—was known as *mamparra*, literally someone who is 'stupid' or who is a fool. A *mamparra* who came back was known as a *magaíça*. The poem is largely about the cultural displacement of these returning miners, and also about how they had sadly exchanged their health and youth for glittering trinkets. When the returning miner gazes at his hand—probably to look at some blemish or skin mark—the allusion is to that dreaded miner's disease, silicosis, a disease of the lungs caused by the inhalation of underground silica dusts.

The Woman who Laughs at Life and Death. To my knowledge, this is the second poem Noémia de Sousa wrote after her thirty-year-long silence. (The other was a poem she composed on the death of Samora Machel.) Writing from her exile in Portugal, she speaks of her assurance that her African origins will be returned to her on death.

RUI KNOPFLI (1932 - 1998)

- *O País dos Outros* (1959)
- *Reino Submarino* (1962)
- *Máquina de Areia* (1964)
- *Mangas Verdes com Sal* (1969)
- *A Ilha de Próspero* (1972)
- *O Escriba Acocorado* (1978)
- *Memória Consentida* (1982) — collected works, 1959-1978
- *Corpo de Atena* (1984)
- *O Monhé das Cobras* (1997)

One of the dominant figures in Mozambican poetry in the period preceding independence, Knopfli studied in Lourenço Marques (Maputo) and in Johannesburg, and he was one of the founders of the influential *Caliban* journal. He published five books of poetry in Mozambique. Knopfli has often been compared (or contrasted) to José Craveirinha: these two poets have been described as the *verso e anverso* (verse and obverse) of Mozambican poetry: they often write about the same things but from altogether different perspectives and using poetic language in a very different manner: Knopfli's diction is elegant and cadenced, and his poems are often full of erudite allusions.

His collection *Corpo de Atena* (1984) won the Portuguese Pen Club Prize for 1985. Although there was some recognition of Knopfli's work in Portugal—and this is especially true of his last book, published shortly before he died—he was generally regarded as something of an outsider. Rui Knopfli worked for the Portuguese Embassy in London from 1975 until shortly before his death in Lisbon.

An Old Poem on the City of Gold [72]*

—1959

In the leaden mornings
of shrill wind
with the lightsome
scent
of blooming orange groves
falling from your hair.
The light tread of the rubber
on the tongue of the tarmac
and the symphony of pylons.
The cold morning of the hills,
buildings, bill-boards
and black men
in grey overcoats
at the street corners of the concrete city.
"Enjoy Rembrandt[†]
and you'll enjoy the masterpiece."
Holdings hands
in the alleyways whose outline
is the light.
Dark-skinned women,
garish berets and glasses.
DRIVE CAREFULLY!
The mild wind
singing in the pylons,
singing,
zum - zumzum,
zumzum - zum
"Any more tickets please,
any more . . . *Asseblief*."[‡]
The outcries whispered in secret,

---

* Johannesburg was often (and still is) referred to as 'the city of gold'.
† South African brand of cigarettes.
‡ *Afk*, 'Please'.

136

the swarm of cars
and the universe of dreams
over our shoulders (it was the time
to dream . . .)
the beauty of the same
journey always
through mounds of yellow dust[§]
screaming to the sky,
Harrison Street
Louis Botha, Jan Smuts.[**]
DAILY MAIL! DAILY MAIL!
A house on top of the hill,
the cold hands,
the scent of orange groves
and the pencil-stroke of black smoke
rising high into the grey sky
of ice and indifference.

[§] The mine dumps around Johannesburg.
[**] Louis Botha and Jan Smuts were central avenues in Johannesburg, both of them
named after Union prime ministers.

Epigram [73]
—1959

Your lips, I tell you, are not as sweet
as honey.

(Too much honey
is sickening.)

But your lips, I tell you, are sweet.
But as sweet as what?
They are as sweet as they are.

Sweet?

Yes, indeed, sweet as is the bread
which we eat every day
and from which we never tire.

Green Mangoes with Salt [74*]
—1969

The faraway taste, the acrid taste
of a childhood shared by a pen-knife
in the wide semi-circle of friendship.

The lingering taste, the enhanced happiness
of the unawares moment, during low-tide,
in that moment of supreme abasement.

The allusive taste that slowly returns
to the bitter palate, the burning mouth,
to the crest of time, half-way through life.

---

* Eating salted green mangoes was a favourite pastime of Mozambican boys.

The Dog of Anguish [75]
—1969

His fur is thinned out and bristly
like that of a dead animal,
sticky slobber drips from his lips
in great glittering strings of foam.
An ancient and resigned wound
lives on in the dim and bloodied gaze.
Wound, for it can longer be a dream,
lacerated by the wrath of a pack of wolves.
He walks, hesitating and unsteady,
under the agonized triangle of the muzzle,
performing a lingering and grotesque dance.
All time is his and there just isn't
time to spare to anyone, O soundless dog,
undercover and shadowy dog,
dog of our pus-engrained hope,
enduring dog, indestructible dog.

Progress [76]
—1969

We are naked like the Greeks in the Acropolis
and the sun staring at us also gazed at them.
Yet when we make love it's with a wrist watch on.

Ariel's Song [77]
—1972

Squalid, spidery shades.
A pitiful sorrow drains itself
all through the length of their thin shoulders.
This way, immobile and mute, riveted
to the walls, the stones, the landscape,
they turn their backs to the dry land,
and, deaf, ignore the din of the world.

They are lost in the range of seas,
and among reflexes of rainbows and suggestions
of sand lies the melancholy gaze of resignation.
What hidden fascination, secret opium,
draws them to the lower coralline?
To what numbed voices, sprung from an abyss,
would they be listening?

The clamour that rises from the mainland
does not disturb or affect them,
in their faces there is no sign, spark
or glow of the fire raging
in the nearby horizon.
Motionless and ancient, they stare at the sea.
These are not the children of Caliban.

The Main Mosque [78*]
—1972

In this low-lying Olympus[†] whose mortar is fever and
the coral reef, I am the greatest God. For as much
as the stones, the walls and the words affirm the
contrary, for as much they tear open my body with the
shape of the cross, for as much as they submit the

arid voice to the inflections of the Latin plainchant,
for as much as the intentions of the small pallid
and yellowed gods chisel the contrary on memorial
stones and their resilience has them as masters, the
blood which spurs the veins of these people

is mine. The emblems in porticos, façades, the metal
of armaments and Power exhibit the arrogance
of your conquerors. Yet the honey of the dates
which moulds the movements of these people,
the chisel that sharpens their wooden profiles,

the slow flame that devours their lean faces,
these are mine. Pained and bloodless, their very
Christ is a Moor from Cabaceira[‡] and he has the
gaunt thinness of an old ascetic dervish.

Race of scribes, command, pronounce, affix:
Only Allah is great and Mohammed is his prophet.

---

[*] The main mosque on the Island of Mozambique.
[†] "In this abode of the gods . . ."
[‡] Settlement on the mainland.

Terrace of Mercy [79]
—1972

Sadly the shadows chant Koranic
verses. White tunics flutter
in the indolence of the warm breeze.
'Old Mercy' feigns to be the masonry

stroked by the whitest *m'siro*,[†] while
along alley-ways and small squares
he pretends to ignore the distant sight of the
green-clad boy from the mosque. Our Father,

Hail Mary, each in time with the black
beads of a rosary carved by Makua[‡]
hands. The withered and parched lips
of the old *patiah*[§] reply, murmuring,
like a medium, the words of the *Gayatri*:[**]

*Tat Savitur vareniam bhargo devasya
dhimahi dhiyo yo nah pracodayat.*
Bewildered heart, kneaded in the clay
of time, what is your true name:

Ghaffaar,[††] Govind[‡‡] or Gonzaga?[§§]

[†] A white paste that women on the Island of Mozambique put on their faces as a sign
of beauty.
[‡] Tribe from the Nampula region, an area which includes the Island of
Mozambique.
[§] Hindu priest or holy man.
[**] A Brahmin mantra or chant.
[††] Al-Ghaffaar, 'The Forgiving' or 'The Forgiver', one of the Ninety-Nine Names of
Allah.
[‡‡] Govind Singh or Govind 'the Lion', the great Sikh spiritual leader.
[§§] Tomás António Gonzaga, 18th century Luso-Brazilian poet who was banished to
the Island of Mozambique, where he started a new career trading in slaves.

Nation ⁸⁰
—1978

A path of loose sand that leads to no particular place.
The trees had names like casuarina, eucalyptus,
Pod Mahogany. The quiet rivers also had names
by which it was custom to designate them. And so had
the birds which flew close against the undergrowth

and the forest, pathway to the blue or the densest
mysterious green that was inhabited by gods and spirits
of a mythology which wasn't even written about in the tomes
and treatises usually devoted to such things. After that,
with the ditches, hills, level ground, and more rivers

that intersected the savannah, the trees, side-paths,
villages, the towns and cities where men lived,
the landscape spread out until even the freak
of an imaginary line was lost from sight. This was what
we called Nation. And from some dark recess

a song sometimes rose up, unpolished and sorrowful,
and the sudden crystal of laughter, the inexplicable
sigh, the mute wantonness of intertwined bodies.
Or the drums of peace pretending to be at war. For this
was never announced in such a distant

and conventional manner. But the blood fertilized
the land, made the heart of the trees shudder
and my brothers, my enemies, were dying. A single
and various languages were spoken and that,
strange as it may seem, we also called Nation.

In place of the four walls there were only stones. With
the sheets of zinc and the timber wounded by many
nailings they made a house. Parts of a dismembered
body thrown to chance, overtaken by the wind and silence,

145

and whose memory—in my case it's residual—

does not survive. I should, perhaps, stand over
the ruins and cry out Nation and childhood, the dead
which preceded its death, the first and final love.
Four walls demolished by chance, which was enough,
in what had been only a world, for the whole world

to enter and the traced-out polygon, while keeping to
its original configuration, would be traversed
by a foreign shiver, a premonition of ice and
winter. Something changes its profile imperceptibly,
sapped by a hidden, persistent sickness.

Similar to any other, that place made the goal
into the point of departure, concepts which, like
the imaginary line, shift around and always elude
the essential. Flanked by shadows and trees, the sand
path which was said to lead to some place opened up

to the world. Experience, however, subsumes the first
statement under the second: no place is reached by
going through the world; fiction and landscape are merely
part of that trivial essence: the legacy of words; Nation
is merely the language in which I express myself.

Cambaco [81*]

Grey, grave, misshapen yet obstinate,
I transport, intact, in my living memory
what needs to be preserved against the ephemeridae
of the swift beasts that jump in my path,
the gracious leaps of the gazelle, the threshed

savannah. In silence I watch them go by
until they eventually disappear, for a moment or, perhaps, forever.
Solitary mastodon in the desolate tableland,
a kind of primitive library, I merely

learnt to be the ultimate guardian
of memory in the couch-grass of the bush.
As for me, I mark my territory with urine,
irregular land-survey of where I am master
and miserly overseer of these meagre spoils.

---

* An old, solitary elephant.

The Indian Snake-Charmer 82

Glorious morning, fixed in the distance,
at the far end of the box of white sand
where, huddled, anonymous and ascetic,
wrapped in white cloths and silence
we find him. A dhoti covers the scrotum

and holds down the thin and wiry legs
of a squalid arachnid. Above, the turban
and the elder's beard sway in the morning breeze.
He begins, then, to bewitch the day
with precise ritual motions. He gets up

at last, the sinuous sound plaintive
and imploring, to reveal, with
slow arabesques, the marvels kept
in the wise wicker basket. Obedient,
the hooded rattlesnakes perform their

act, in style they cover up the deceitful painting.
Damp, their swift, glittering and fatal
bifid tongues dart in the sun.
We, children, paralyzed by fear
and amazement. The mat would be lost

to us far into the sand, threadbare flying carpet
airborne, immobile, in the deep sky
of the imagination. Privileged observer
of this fierce vigil which is now, very meekly,
annexed by the shores of slumber

Notes

An Old Poem on the City of Gold. Of all Mozambican poets Rui Knopfli is one who is the most familiar with day-to-day life in South African and the workings of the apartheid system. The days of his young adulthood spent in Johannesburg left him with a love for kwela jazz. It also left him with a life-long distaste for white South African liberals; for example, when our first Nobel laureate was awarded her prize he had this to say in a Portuguese newspaper: "God save us from South African liberals."[83] His poems about Johannesburg in the mid-1950s are altogether lacking in the optimism of liberals; it is as if, looking at South Africa from the outside, he could better see the level of indifference in a society, that compared to Mozambique, was so highly mechanized that it had become itself like a mighty machine. Knopfli could well foresee that the machine would endure for a lot longer than people hoped it would. Despite all this, the love for the people of South Africa is self-evident.

The Dog of Anguish & **Progress**. These poems should perhaps be read in conjunction with Craveirinha's "Civilization" and "Cell Number One". Knopfli was aware that representing injustice in poetry is an endeavour that is riddled with dangers: rage at the injustice can be so overwhelming that it can obscure the actual 'meaning' of the poem—and this sort of criticism would be valid for a poem, like, say, Craveirinha's "Communiqué from Cuíto Cuanavale"—or, else, the portrayal of injustice may be used to evoke pity or other similar messy sentiments; at worst, these things may make a poem read like a sing-song of woes and lamentation. But whether Knopfli's elegant and allusive diction is an appropriate medium to convey or represent injustice is an altogether different question.

Ariel's Song. The poem is ostensibly about a group of old men on the Island of Mozambique—the island that has given the country its name— who gaze at the sea, oblivious to the tumult in the continent. But the poem is also significant in that it raises important questions about nationhood and language. The 'ancient men' in the poem who gaze nostalgically at the sea—at the land beyond the sea? the motherland? Portugal?—cannot be considered true Mozambicans: "These are not the children of Caliban." The figure of Caliban, derived from Shakespeare's *The Tempest*, has been much used in the context of Mozambican literature. *Caliban* was the title of a literary journal, edited by Knopfli, which appeared in the early 1970s. The figure of Caliban in the poem is perhaps better understood in terms of opposition to Prospero, who can be read to stand for the Master Language, or for cultural or imperialist domination. Caliban, the silenced slave, appropriates the language of his master and uses it as his own. We have here, in symbolic form, the linguistic situation of Mozambicans, obliged, by nature of historical circumstance, to speak Portuguese, yet making it their own. The poem is taken from a collection called *Ilha de Próspero* (Prospero's Island).

The Main Mosque & Terrace of Mercy. These are two poems about the Island of Mozambique and the cultures that coexist there. The first poem shows how, even though the Portuguese conquerors brought with them the Christian religion, the people remained obdurately Islamic; the poem can be read as an elegant tribute to Islam, this coming from a man whose background was Christian. (The Islamic theme is taken up in the poems Luís Carlos Patraquim wrote about the Island of Mozambique, and Ana Mafalda Leite's more recent versions.) The second poem is an polyphonic composition where we can hear the voices of the two other main religions on the island—Christianity and Hinduism—and also, indirectly, Islam. The poem is really a dialogue between a Catholic layman praying the rosary and a Brahman priest chanting the Gayatri.

Nation. This is Rui Knopfli's great poem of exile. It is a poem about the Nation that had once been. The poem diligently portrays the country that had been experienced as Nation: it traverses the country, its characteristic landscapes, the houses; it gives short summaries of its history, customs, lore, things which had been the poet's heritage, his erstwhile space. The sense is that the Nation, the real one, the one traversed in the poem, has been lost. When, in very dismissive manner, the poem says ". . . Nation / is merely the language in which I express myself" the allusion is to famous saying attributed to the Portuguese poet, Fernando Pessoa: "My Nation is the Portuguese language". The suggestion, at once cosmopolitan, is also one of no commitment to a particular place or country. 'Nation' has now become the means by which poetry gets to be expressed, the language which conveys the poetry; the other Nation, the nation of childhood, has been lost, and with it all innocence.

RUI NOGAR (1935 - 1993)

- *Silêncio Escancarado* (1982)

The poet made a mark for himself as anti-colonial poet already at a young age. In 1965 he was jailed by the PIDE, the security police of Portugal's fascist regime. After independence, he continued to produce works hailing the construction of a new society. Rui Nogar published only one book during his lifetime. He died in Lisbon.

The Alligator [84]
—1976

is
an ugly animal
repugnant   repulsive
ultra-dangerous and pseudo-drowsy

this saurian
is a lethargic lizard
as is colono-culturalism

long jaws
armed with saws
always sharp
always ready to prove to us
that there's a law
that'll be giving
continuity
to their species
at the expense of other species

he comes
from a species
on the way to extinction
but which we
with this craze
to protect others
but never ourselves
keep on maintaining
to the rhythm of ecological equilibrium

but beware
he is treacherous

he never defies
the destiny of others

unless it is
inside his own habitat

eco-ego-centric
that's what he is
and he loves the metatarsal bone
of those who make
the wrong move
and the knotty phalanxes
of the incautious washerwomen

he's also an animal
with a tendency for grandeur
a megalomaniac
he's out there
alluring the bourgeoisie
he's made into shoes and handbags
at prices only
a parasitic class could afford

exorbitant
that's how he got
to align himself
with the enemy.

and being irrational by nature
he always lives for far too long

it's necessary to liquidate him
and the sentence is to take effect
while he is still small

with its milk-teeth
and the treachery
still inside the husk of intentions

yes
and we ought to extend this
defensive strategy
to many other animals

for example   lice
blood-sucking leeches   bugs
and other such fascists

the permanent enemies
of our ideological species

Time [85]

I'm from the time
when a black man
      with money
       was a thief
a black man without money
       a vagrant
a black man without a boss
       was a thief
a black man with a boss
       was lazy
a well-dressed black dude
       Look at the guy
       he thinks he's somebody
a humble illiterate black man
       You poor devil
       you're not worth a thing

I'm from the time
when a black man
       without the letter of consent
       with the boss' signature
       to go out into the street
       to go to school
       to be somebody
       outside the home or the backyard
       after the curfew at 21 hundred
       was sure to get arrested
       to spend life doing work
       there on the cotton fields
       there on the islands of São Tomé*
       there on the docks there on the mines
       there in the graves he's nobody's man

---

* The island archipelago of São Tomé and Príncipe in the Gulf of Guinea; many Mozambicans were 'recruited' to work on the cocoa plantations on the islands.

and there'll be no family to know about it
but I am also
from the time
when it was we who began to
force other
to become men
or to be white

HELIODORO BAPTISTA (1944 -)

- *Por Cima de Toda a Folha* (1987)
- *A Filha de Thandi* (1991)
- *Nos Joelhos do Silêncio* (2005)

The poet belongs to the new generation of poets who made their name in the period after independence. He is a journalist in the city of Beira. Heliodoro Baptista was awarded Mozambique's National Poetry Prize in 1991. His poetry seems to contradict the belief that committed poetry consists of easy slogans and repeated catch-phrases; Baptista's poetry is, if anything, opaque and difficult.

The Village [86]
—1973

(*on the massacre at Wiriyamu**)

I
Behold
the friendliness of the mornings
expressing themselves so well
in the bombed-out space.

And everything purifies itself,
while on the surface
a difficult sun reclines
southerly in our anguish,
like these glittering birds
pecking out on the self-satisfied debris.

The cities fade
into the background with combat gear
cutting a profile against the tropical winds.
It's from them that depart the
the migratory flights of motors
and the facsimiled azimuths
of the professionals.

Only now is it perceptible
because the romantic light melts
the myopic horror of the stars
—from which comes the light
which forebodes guilt.

II

---

* Site of a massacre of innocent villagers by the Portuguese colonial army. The massacre occurred between the 16th and 18th of December 1972. The eye-witness accounts of the massacre, first collected by missionary priests in Mozambique. The international outcry that followed had a lot to do with the sheer cold-blooded viciousness of the tortures which the soldiers had devised to inflict on the villagers.

Yet the mornings are so amiable
in the village which doesn't stir
and which has no words within it.
Screams no longer return
as screams. And in the grass
only the black flower of its memory
waves at us from the dusk
which is inscribed in the poem.

Once again the rotations of dust
give colour to the horizon,
while under the impartial countenance of the clouds
a pitch-black angel patiently cleans
the golden sweat of the propellers.

III
When we can't sleep
we'll quickly call for
the irreplaceable circles.
We will rise, groping
for the fragmented vehemence
of these made dead
in their prime.

Yet in the air
at each withdrawal into weariness
the village, house by house,
filters through the black-market of the cells
(of each spiritless heart)
the liberated eternity
in the mouth of the one who did not betray.

And primordial muscles
coming from the walk of praise,
their eyes on the fire,
are hushed into
and become comrades of the proverb:

"If the sky has feelings
it's because it has become old."

The Other Hands

> It's strange to think that
> here no one knows anything at all
> Juan Carlos Onetti

The hands of power, my love,
are human hands.

Be they full of rapid movements, rough, smooth,
fat, excitable, rain-wet,
they remain human hands.

We are seduced by gods or myths,
even by the horror staring us in the face,
but those things merely represent
the lightest of all things within space.

Apart from these hands, my love, there are others
which dig into the pulses already bereft of life,
and their movement corrupts everything,
in the same way the bad breath of the hyena
ruins the pose of the beautiful and skilled lion
when it pounces on its prey.

Yet they remain human,
these hands that prevent the blood from pumping
vital things like love
and other things that demand to be named.

But what these hands have committed
is a manual for history
(along the lines of standardized reports),
I say it without pain
to the vessels of communication
of some of our clever-versed
contemporaries.

What is important now is to gauge
the emotional-charge of the glands
and to retain the genuine fakir's
holy discipline of will.

These wise hands, the other hands,
will build stars right here
on the ashes of the dream that has survived
—the true-to-life firefly
that points to our readiness
to be clients
of any future.

Mayakovsky [88]

Never did a full gunshot
give so much happiness
to the professionally weary
and the acrobats of intrigue.

Even though he was rehabilitated
by the death he opted for
he continues to spread confusion,
the chill of the razor blade
on the dictatorship of routine.

"Let us rise then, poet,
to the height of eagles,
let us sing
above all the hairdos in the world."

Love insists on the freedom of pores
and that's the wise paradox
all the generations learn
so they can sing in verse.

To a Naïve Nordic Woman [89]
—1989

Continue collecting kangas
of historical interest
but don't mark them with the sweat
of your Saxon presence,
but rather with the certainties
which are put into doubt
by the insecurity of your progressiveness
inhabited by talismans
and penises from many nations.

Pronounce your R's and give them that incurable
evocation of hidden pretexts
when, in the aseptic refuge of your room,
you exorcise ghosts
whilst you use men,
valuable items who hold, always,
the secret of the means
to achieve some aim.

Use everything in pursuit of a CV:
language with which to sail,
your whole body as a bait.
Watch out for your evasiveness
and dedicate yourself
to any alternative.

Learn, still, to make *matapa**
and in your memory
humbly keep or learn
the names of some rivers,
half-a-dozen wild animals.

---

* A typical Mozambican dish made with coconut milk, crushed peanuts, vegetables
and seafood.

Having put the disgust aside,
savour, if you can, the pleasure of lying supine,
because the experience will endure for longer
than your naïve talismans.

This way, make the time you have spent with us
the ultimate exercise in intimate passion,
the unbreakable bond
of the genuine orgasm.

[Translated with Maria de Lourdes Magalhães]

MARIA MANUELA de SOUSA LOBO (1946 -)

One of the most original experimental poets to have appeared in the period following independence, Maria Manuela de Sousa Lobo has yet to collect her poems in book form. She studied at the Universidade Eduardo Mondlane in Maputo. She left Mozambique in 1988. She now teaches Portuguese as a Foreign Language in Lisbon and lives in Sintra.

Magaíça-Kid 90*
—1973

1.
he brought in his left hand that reddish mark
of the claws of the panther,
the scales from a different calmness,
the face of someone strangled by his own hands
—oh how it is beautiful—

and he walked, gazing at the ravaged fields, rivers,
mountains and volcanoes, green grass
oh lava of blood and lymph and plasma and wound—oh land
sown with entrails and with the water-silence
of a gaze erased by killing fountains

The eyes of my magaíça-kid, so wide-awake, listening
two eyes to look upon the sea
in the vastness of the struggle
and fixed upon the distant sight of some white sail

he left like the cold spotted lizards
with their entrails flattened
against the whitewash of the walls

2.
and he walked along that path of solitude and silicosis†
nice boots   a peacock feather   a gold watch

who removed the lungs of my giant friend David?
hanging from a ring in the ear
is the red cage of a humming-bird out in the sun

---

* A *magaíça* is a Mozambican miner who has returned home after having worked in
the Witwatersrand gold mines in South Africa.
† A disease of the lungs caused by the inhalation of underground silica dusts;
essentially, a miner's disease.

who will sell me lungs with less blood
so I can give them to my friend?
ah   who will fill up
the artery which is so lonesome
and white and thin

a thin drop of silicosis
continues to varnish the bent nail
of this path of dust,
the boots of the deceased,
all ire to Goliath who is also poor
and who dies in the same wasteland of this mine

[Translated with Maria de Lourdes Magalhães]

Two Unkind Anti-Sonnets [91]
—1975

> *there's no xicuembo*
> *there's only our strength*
> *September 75*

1.

it wasn't because of you   falcon*   we felt subdued
that my mother cried   I buried my aunt
children   palm trees   roasted by napalms of lava
my lonesome daughter   cold   frozen by the falcon

after the scorching over Mueda[†]   grains
yeah it wasn't because of you   no   that we made
our Kalasha[‡] speak   it spoke   was speaking
the light   moon   cried   my naked woman

we went on foot   there's no *xicuembo*[§]
you eat mealie meal** not chick peas (no comrade no)
O crooked cactus   O sister spear

in our inspired bushveld there's only our strength
rats   baboons   a thousand thousand and a thousand
arrows   Kalasha will speak for you   it will make Pah

2.

we are monkeys on the willow branches
that the elephant   friend   takes in his trunk
we shout yes   motherless   we shout unsilenced
we shout   grenaded   machine-gunned   dust

---

* A *falcão* (falcon) was the name given, during colonial times, to a Portuguese army helicopter that landed in the middle of the night.
† A town in Northern Mozambique, near Tanzania, site of one of the earliest massacres by the colonial state.
‡ Automatic Kalashnikov (AK47).
§ *Xi-Ronga*, sorcery.
** *SAfr Eng*, maize meal or porridge.

earthworms   snakes   we are ants hanging
over Nyassa   lakes   lunar lizards
we shout the singular freeze after the scorching
we say no vulture   plane   falcon

we are rats   thousands   granaries   burrows
a thousand coconut trees with lengthy shades in the bush
a thousand rabbits   two thousand betrayed teeth

there's no *xicuembo*   there's no pheasant   there's none
we're four thousand grasshoppers jumping from the bells
millions of closed fists   there's only our strength

[Translated with Maria de Lourdes Magalhães]

LUÍS CARLOS PATRAQUIM (1953 -)

- *Monção* (1982)
- *A Inadiável Viagem* (1985)
- *Vinte e Tal Novas Formulações e uma Elegia Carnívora* (1991)
- *Mariscando Luas* (1992) — with Ana Mafalda Leite & Roberto Chichorro
- *Lindenburgo Blues* (1998)
- *O Osso Côncavo e Outros Poemas* (2005) — collected works

Probably the most important poet to have appeared after independence, Luís Carlos Patraquim has been seen by many as Craveirinha's worthy successor in the poetic fusion of public and private concerns, the metaphorically-charged diction, and the handling of particularly complex themes. He is a poet whose work has become progressively more difficult—tighter in structure, more allusive—with each coming book. He left Mozambique in 1986 and now lives in Loures, in Portugal. He was awarded Mozambique's National Poetry Prize in 1995.

Metamorphosis [92]

to the poet José Craveirinha

I was still small
when fear drew wax-shine from the city
      see, I didn't even own a coat
and neither did I have a feeling for this grave world
and nor had I read Carlos Drummond de Andrade[*]

the acacias burst open in their secret joy of being pods
and red flowers
and there wasn't even wax-shine
      (so I'd know about it)
on infancy's wooden floors
in the house

Mother wasn't yet a woman
and afterwards became Mother
      and it is woman who is the pod and the earth
then I understood colour
and metaphor

but now   with Adamastor[†] dead
      you saw the scurvy in him and sang the dawn
      of spitting mambas in the tracks of the bush
let's talk of coats and fear
drumming the sound and the words
over the green plains
and the bronzed stalks
      the lattices no longer tremble, no they don't
      and the 7th of March[‡] is now called June,
      ever since a day, a long while ago,

---

[*] The Brazilian modernist poet.
[†] The 'spirit of the Cape' in Camões' *Os Lusíadas*.
[‡] The city square called 7 de Março (7th of March) was renamed 25 de Junho (25th of June), Mozambican independence day.

171

with half a dozen Mozambican ruffians
                    all of them poets
        drawing the chalk outline of nature and the ground
        under a Parnassus[§] of bullets
let's talk of the dawn and the day's dying
because the monsoon has come
and the last of the insomniacs fills the night
with teeming thoughts,
the tisane of desire in a silence of frogs

        while the ones that strum at the guitar
                    with their castor oil and peanut tins
        gently tap the other tendons of memory
        and concretely
        the music is the play-thing

                                    the ring

                                            and the dream

        of children who look at coats and laugh
        in this shameless innocence of a morning gleam
        that you
        clandestinely planted
        WITH GREAT SHOUTS

[§] In Greek mythology, the home of the muses and Apollo; the source of inspiration of poets.

"I draw the curtains of the afternoon . . ." [93]

I draw the curtains of the afternoon
because I desire your fullness
within the poem

you go past in your kanga
and your body is like the dunes
where the pine trees
that rustle nearby grow

you brandish the fury
of the falling wave
in my gesture

"I think of your hands as gills inside the sea . . ." [94]

"the world rests entirely on your eyes"
Paul Éluard

I think of your hands as gills inside the sea
your hands that breathe sounds
and I think I'm within a shoal of moving fish
all things I see are islands in movement
and you appear, new-founded country,
stripped naked of all leaves,
rising from the land of shifting obsessions
to the multi-coloured pulse
with which the tendons are spurred
O what gills that do not breathe, your hands
that drive the river into wildness
and carve out the geography of the world

Song

I will come with the trees
(my love) with the sound of blood
inside the cathedrals of pure touch
with the scream and the sea-
birds inside the very syllables
into that short-lived climax of foam
hands on your hands I will come

I will come with swords
green belt of sand in the plains
into the marrow (my love) of hunger
with fruit in your eyes
beloved wind that's waiting
into the world's nucleus of sex
nerve into water I will come

I will come on the mornings sweaty
with the voice (my love) that was liberated
into the nocturnal billow of the poem
with birds inside the scream
or even a remote sea echo
into the minute root of crystals
death to meet your death I will come

I will come standing on my feet
into the silence that is drained into rivers
I row to the sound of dazzled songs
with you into the beginning I will come

Indian Ocean Ode 96

robber of the wind and the fragile
Indian Ocean lines that spurt
in clear partying / with my blood
I scarf what I can / untameable
geometry of caves in this

sea / Khayyam* vintage wine / drop
all the way to spasm in the rim where I insert
my cedilla when the beloved moves to and fro /

for the Pleiades come from within her
with the scream of daybreak
and wet birds sarong her
tuft / salty rhythm of the monsoons

---

* Omar Khayyam, the author of the *Rubaiyát*.

Carnivorous Elegy [97]
—1986

> "Because I do not hope to turn again"
> TS Eliot, *Ash-Wednesday*

In memory of Samora Machel

because they make us into neatly-packaged bundles of flesh
hurled into the night, I howl in blood
into god's sluggish shadows on the road,
because we're fast into the night now
—and we don't drowse like dogs anymore—
a few of us return, hidden among god's
shadows, a name in Tsalala.[*]
At one in the morning we are gods
whip-lashed against the outline of the houses,
the temples pulsating with the flights
of exhausted birds and we knock on the poem. Open!
We no longer die under the hands
of the playing two-year-old child.
He killed himself so he couldn't be man or god,
or even questions that like flights portend
useless metaphysics on Sunday's daybreak,
at one in the morning.
Mother, I want a smiling green boat
and a river inside the bones and a tarred road
of clean flesh, without god's leftovers
or the night slobbering up in the mouth, Mother!

Let us knock. Open the magnificent stadiums
inside every orifice! Spit on us
with the fire that kills. Open!
At one in the morning, my god.
So few of us in the South, clean and far away

---

[*] Peri-urban zone in Maputo, target of many attacks by the armed bandits.

177

from the land of Hyperboreans.[†] They've got
nothing now and a large heart of ideas
is rotting in the wrenched groins.
We return, in that lost gasp of ours,
we who lose our way—god's
matricide/suicide in the rubbish heap—
with gang-man videos that set our style
into electric rainbow-coloured ulcers.
Give us our lungs black-marketed in Tsalala,
the ululating Polana[‡]-spasms in those
mass meetings—wedding feasts!—
in the public square over the gums of our days!
We demand everything: the very viscera of the wind;
the biblical intricacy in the cunt hairs
of glittering naked psalms; and god's vomit also
and fear and rage and blood and dogs
and stuttering dead abortions, O my god
nocturne-vagina-mother, slipping into the *chigubo*'s[§]
awaiting bayonets of ecstasy!
At one in the morning, my neatly-packaged bundle
of country, machine-gunned flesh of this poem.

Silence. I embrace an agonized body
of intermittent, assassinated words.
Look at the guts of all the gods
strangling us. What fragrance is that shit
which they set for us on the first night?
In what black holds were those old-time animals?
Where did the mahoganies drown?
Who in Tsalala sobs to himself a name
that's made of semen and salt?
What do we return as?
At one in the morning, my god.
Behold the scrotum sac; the shoulders tired
of holding the world, the rhythmic sounds

[†] In Greek mythology, the land beyond the north wind, the home of the terrible
gorgons.

[‡] Up-market suburb in Maputo.

[§] The 'chigubo', *Xi-Ronga*, is a praise dance performed before or after a battle.

178

in tales of hyenas, the haemorrhage of fear
in the eyes of the cane, the memory of the land
sucking itself in the avenged aortas.
My god of all of us, why do we return without
the two-year-old child? For he was no packaged bundle
to idle away among the veins of an iron sky,
and not just the flesh of the poem devouring itself in a scream.
At one in the morning.
The crickets glint like glass over flowers
in this night that came from a night of silence
for we return, howl from howl,
from the multiplying succubus which we aren't
but are and which begot us.

ALL POEMS WERE SHOT BY A FIRING SQUAD.

"Island, body, woman . . ." [98]

Island,[*] body, woman. Island, enchantment. The first theme to be sung. The first attempt to see you: in the tired flesh of the outward fortress, in the rigid corrugation of the derelict house, thinking out memories, slaves, corals, saffron. My island/vulva of fire and stone forgotten in the Indian Ocean. I sail around you, from the frizzled hair of the rock to the heaving womb, and I sculpt you with the blue and the sun. You: thatch released into the Orient, always exiled from yourself.

---

[*] The Island of Mozambique.

"You were, at one time . . ." [99]

You were, at one time, mercantile sumptuousness, unattainable courtesan with garments trailing against the high walls of palaces. Over the Arabic blossom, the excision sketched with names from far. The palace of São Paulo. Sixteenth century fate of "arms and distinguished men".[*] São Paulo and the gunpowder of the Gospels in the cannons of the galleons. Rose-pink São Paulo, ebony, blood, the singing of crystals, doublets and swords, the heaving of voices in fleeting recesses. Will the ghosts really sleep in the cobblestone grooves, with the tower reciting the lamentations? My gentle souls of cloths and glass beads, who stopped you from giving birth with the brick that remained and grew old?

Island, kanga imprinted with soldiers and death. Elegiac island of monuments. Aircraft-carrier with the crows of premonitions at the juncture of the monsoons. From east to east you scourged the inland. From Calicut to Lisbon, the spear which was made to quaver into nocturnal, sporadic duels by the lewd wind and doubt which has now re-translated itself somewhere between belfry and minaret. Exalted muezzin, unconquerable.

Because in the beginning there was the sea and the Island. Sinbad and Ulysses. Scheherazade and Penelope. Names over names. Tongue from tongues, multiple matricide in Makua.

---

[*] The opening words of Camões' *Os Lusíadas*.

Dis-sonnet ¹⁰⁰
—1996

Death will flee away from me
with such zeal and such fury
that when I see her, affronted,
eagerly offering herself to some other,

or in gold, milk and all the flesh
cutting through the livid portico
or biting the propped-up navel
of the Fates or of luscious Venus,

I will always be the restless dog
barking fine sand inside the bud
of pubic hair, the prodigal hard-on

which thinks of her as the only lasting mystery,
greater than the shout, the fear, the spawning
which is transfigured through her.

extracts from **Lydenburg Blues**[101]
—1996

I
It's where the Island returns at the end of the tracks of herdsmen,
the reed house, fragile, pliable,
in the osteoporosis of a column that chirps, *tchaia,*[*]
between the occipital and the coccyx; a murmuring
—*bloody river!*—
and the wheels of the Great Trek.
I saw the name, it was beautiful from high in the guava tree,
the scolopendras, rainbow-decked, alive in the hands,
and the crippled shell of the green bus swallowed up
by the distance of being
and in the far, far distance
—' it's not because of this it bleeds'
the *Amêjoe*!![†] . . . slow, now like a blind scream,
a column of wind where we can write out the silence.

Ein jerder Engel ist schrecklich, *passop!*[‡]
Beware, you, the one that sees the spirit of the Night
and the ethereal albinos fading into the rustling
tree-tops of the mango trees. They—the accursed—
keep watch on the city and disembowel the Leopard.
They sleep in the tongue of the Snake.

'Lindenburgh', you used to say,
over the veins of the palm leaves.
Raised up high, sustaining the aorta,
rods of god's skin caressing the lungs.

Nomadic address! You're always with me
through my journeys everywhere.

---

[*] To hit or to make a sound.
[†] The ritual cry of cockle-sellers, a corruption of the Portuguese *amêijoa* (cockle).
[‡] *SAfr Eng*, 'watch out!'

Temple irrigated by blood, I hail you!
When the mist clothes the melancholy fields
and fever is hurled over the houses,
I walk ahead
towards the impossible shadow.

A bellyful of the fruit of the loquat,
that is my path, wrinkled like an old man's face
and hanging from memory and I jump over a wall,
I steal, I savour the fruit
in that uncovered incarnation over the tarmac.

This end-directed water, the here and now
of the least happenings. The regal hood of the blue lizard,
the long and shrewd tongue over the kanga,
and the buds of exposed flesh, the frenetic gift of the flower.
And the hum of the winged ants after the rain
laying out a cloak of dead silk, such a high
spirit, so short-lived!

On the wall I finish up the nipple of the green mango,
the milk like the fright
of the first wank sprinkling the leaves
of the mahogany, tree-gum giving scent to the afternoon.

When the ship is swallowed up by the dark breath
of the Night still to come,
whose presage is the furious tail of the gecko
that had been stoned
and, untiring, rests over the Head
of the world all around the hands.
I write the House of fire, the terrifying Bird,
the curve of the Saddle, the flight towards the Name!

Notes

Metamorphosis. The poem is a tribute to José Craveirinha, who was already, by this stage, the grand old man of Mozambican letters. It alludes to Craveirinha's prison poems, "Wax-Shine", "Our City", and "Metamorphosis". The allusive appropriation of the Mozambican poetic tradition, of its many voices and styles, will become an important feature of Luís Carlos Patraquim's poetic discourse; here we see it at its incipient stage. The poem exults in the new (post-revolutionary) political order and in particular it praises Craveirinha's role in creating a poetic work that, while it recorded the injustices of the colonial system, also looked forward to the change-over to a new order. Patraquim uses the image of Adamastor to represent the Portuguese colonial imperialist project. Adamastor was 'the spirit of the Cape' in *Os Lusíadas* [The Lusiads], the Portuguese Renaissance epic poem. Craveirinha's role in speaking out against this scurvy-ridden Adamastor is conveyed in the very African image of spitting snakes that herald the new dawn: "you saw in him the scurvy and sang the dawn / of spitting mambas in the tracks of the bush". (It is a different vision of Adamastor from that evident in the poetry of, say, Roy Campbell, a poet who did much to make the figure of Adamastor better known in the English-speaking world.) The new order is compared to a monsoon (the title also of Patraquim's first collection), the wet season of replenishment and sexual awakening, source of what Patraquim "the tisane of desire". The monsoon is clearly the right time to be in. Significantly, this new order, the 'monsoon that has come', derives much from the efforts of poets in creating a language, a discourse, that prepared people for this change. There is a clear references to how many of the leaders of the armed struggle had been poets: "with half a dozen Mozambican ruffians / all of them poets / drawing the chalk outline of nature and of ground / under a Parnassus of bullets". Looking back now we see that many of these noble-minded people were unfortunately also minor poets; perhaps it was an unconscious slip that made Patraquim refer to them as 'ruffians'. The greatest praise is however reserved for José Craveirinha, the one who had toiled in the recesses of the night towards creating the "shameless innocence of . . . [this] morning gleam".

"I draw the curtains of the afternoon . . ." In the work of Patraquim sexual desire is linked to the notion of poetic creation. The poem, more than simply a text, is the centre of upheaval; the poem is itself a place of desire:

"I desire your fullness / within the poem". This is because the monsoon occurs also within the poem; it permeates its texture and determines its sound patterns: ". . . the scream and the sea-birds / [are] inside the very syllables" writes Patraquim in another poem. The poem is a place where things occur, a site of revelation, of experience and epiphany.

"I think of your hands as gills inside the sea . . ."; Song & Indian Ocean Ode. One of the interesting developments of the post-75 period was the appearance of poetic texts that spoke primarily of love; lyrically-charged, sometimes highly allusive, this poetry was also singularly hermetic in quality. The hermetic quality of his poetry was criticized at the time for being 'decadent' or 'bourgeois', which is to say, for turning away from 'social realist poetry' which seemed, to many, to be the 'correct' poetry in that post-revolutionary climate of national reconstruction. Yet the allusive texture of Patraquim's poetry, its coded references, seem appropriate to a kind poetry that speaks of erotic concerns. Sometimes these erotic poems make concessions to the prevalent ideology by using the language of the struggle and national reconstruction to talk about the sexual; the beloved, for example, is compared to the "new-founded country", that is, the independent nation. Images of the country, its rivers, its geography, are likewise used to express the sexual act, as well as the scale and dimension of the sensual experience: "O what gills that do not breathe, your hands/ that drive the river into wildness / and carve out the geography of the world".

Carnivorous Elegy. The civil war which erupted in Mozambique needs to be seen in the context of the creation of a Marxist-Leninist state in Southern Africa. It is obvious, given the Cold War politics of the time, that the new state would have many enemies, externally as well as internally. The erosion of traditional tribal structures, internal discontentment and power struggles within FRELIMO, the presence of many fiercely anti-communist rightwing white Mozambicans in exile, especially in South Africa, and the apartheid regime's antagonism to a Marxist-Leninist state on its borders, the convergence of all these factors was to prove to be especially lethal. Armed banditry, initiated by RENAMO (acronym for Mozambican National Resistance), aided by German, American and Portuguese right-wingers, and supported by South Africa, soon got out of control. Armed banditry became a self-generating machine, one where, so often, a victim became the perpetrator of the next wave of violence. Children were often forcibly inducted into violence by being forced to kill their parents. The stories of atrocities are indeed savage. One of the signs of banditry was to cut off parts

186

of the body. Dismemberment became an emblem of the war. This poem about the war is dedicated to the memory of Samora Machel (the Mozambican President who died in an aeroplane accident in South Africa in 1987). It does not seem, on reading the poem, the sort of thing any leader would want to have dedicated to him, for it is a poem of an extraordinary violence: "We no longer die under the hands/ of the playing two year-old child / He killed himself so he couldn't be man or god". (Many Mozambicans took the dedication to mean that it was precisely Samora Machel's political mistakes in the 1970s that were at the origins of the war, and in some way he should be blamed for the chaos which was to engulf the country. The poem is both an elegy on his death and an elegy for the country he had devoured or the country that had been devoured.) The language of the poem is full of deliberately grotesque metaphors, "stuttering dead abortions", "bayonets of ecstasy", "the veins of an iron sky", "god's matricide/suicide in the rubbish heap". These metaphors suggest an almost unnatural upheaval in the order of things. The very style of the poem replicates the violence assailing the country. Here we must remember Patraquim's conception, which I have previously developed, that the poem is a place where something occurs. The representational space, the phonological patterns and the syntax, do more than inscribe the violence, they are sites of extraordinary violence on the fabric of language, on this "neatly-packaged bundle / of country, machine-gunned flesh of this poem".

"You were, at one time . . ." This is a highly allusive prose poem about the island-city of Mozambique. The Island is seen as the meeting place of many cultures: it is the space "between belfry and minaret", between the Arabic-Islamic culture and the Western-Christian one which superseded it, although it did not abolish or obliterate it: "Over the Arabic blossom, the excision sketched with names from far." One of these names is the constantly repeated 'São Paulo', which means 'St Paul', and refers to the pink-coloured palace of São Paulo ('St Paul's Palace'), the official residence of the governor during the time that the Island of Mozambique was the capital of the country we now call Mozambique. The pink palace stands, in other words, for the Portuguese colonial enterprise, its conquerors, and its inheritance. This is also how we should read the constant references to Luís de Camões, who is said to have completed *Os Lusíadas*, during his stay at the Island of Mozambique. The line that speaks of the sixteenth-century "fate of arms and distinguished men" is a clear borrowing from *Os Lusíadas*, which begins with the rather Virgilean *As armas e os barāoes assinaladas* [lit. The arms and distinguished men]. There is also reference to a famous sonnet by Camões, which is said to been addressed to the poet's deceased Chinese lover: *Alma minha gentil, que te partiste / Tão cedo desta vida, descontente* [lit. My gentle soul, banished / So soon from this life, so full of woe]. The beloved or the 'gentle soul' in the sonnet by Camões is transformed into something that suggests the trafficking of goods and mercantile rapaciousness: "My gentle souls of cloths and glass beads". The colonialist enterprise is rightly seen as a mixture of war, religion, trade, as "the gunpowder of the gospels in the cannons of the galleons". But the island was more than a trade depot, it was also a slave port. "From east to east you scourged the inland." It was from the island that slave raids were launched into the interior. The first slave raiders were the Arabs with their Islamic culture; then came the Portuguese, whose culture was Western and, consequently, moulded by the Hellenic matrix that has shaped Western culture. The conquerors, first the Arabic-Islamic, then the Hellenic-Western, brought their tongues and their stories, superseding those that had been there before. Those who were there first were the Makua people. The *motherland* of the Makua becomes the site of a multiple matricide: "Because in the beginning there was the sea and the Island. Sinbad and Ulysses. Scheherazade and Penelope. Names over names. Tongue from tongues, multiple matricide in Makua."

Dis-sonnet. Even though many of the poems by Patraquim derive much of their force from coded references to other poems he has written, we must not assume that what we have before us is a private language. The poems also utilize a whole repertoire of traditional associations; death, for example, has a long lineage as a reference to an orgasm, as in the French expression *la petite mort*, 'the little death'. To make sense of this poem it is necessary to have these traditional associations in mind. Expressions such as 'dog' and 'bud' are, likewise, traditional metaphors.

Lydenburg Blues. The poem is an evocation of the poet's childhood and of the street where he grew up. 'Rua Lidemburgo' (Lydenburg Street) was named after the one-time Boer Republic of Lydenburg. It was the road that led to the Transvaal. The Voortrekkers who had settled in Delagoa Bay (to be renamed Lourenço Marques, and then later Maputo) left on this road, hence the references to the 'wheels of the Great Trek' and 'bloody river' (cf. the battle of Blood River). The poem alludes also to the other—imaginary?—'Lindenburgh' and it is in this context that an excerpt from the first of Rilke's "Duino Elegies" is cited: *Ein jerder Engel ist schrecklich* (Every angel is terrible).

ANA MAFALDA LEITE (1956 -)

- *Em Sombra Acesa* (1984)
- *Canções de Alba* (1989)
- *Mariscando Luas* (1992) — with Luís Carlos Patraquim & Roberto Chichorro
- *Rosas da China* (2000)
- *Passaporte do Coração* (2002)
- *Livro das Encantações* (2005)

One of those poets that canon-makers find easier to ignore than to categorize, Ana Mafalda Leite cannot be placed too firmly within either the Mozambican or Portuguese poetic traditions. It is probably more advisable to see her as belonging to both traditions, enriching both with her highly original gift. She did her schooling in Lourenço Marques (Maputo) and completed her university training in Lisbon. A teacher of Lusophone African literature—she is a professor at the University of Lisbon—her work attests also to a self-reflexive poetic reworking of that tradition.

The Sailor's First Speech 102

I glance at the last waving boat from this land I bid farewell

I am silence which moves without aim into a centre
which is decentred of all murmurs
my heart is a deranged admiral and the boat is already
other than this   I follow no direction   the soul wanders
the mistake is nothing but the swerve over the swerve
—boundless direction—

I am what I don't remember
slender figure that slips away into mists of sand
I make and unmake myself and when the winds arrive over the sea
my soul is already scattered dust
being nothing I ask for nothing   I meditate
and nothingness allows my destiny to be complete
boundless sea oh sea! sea and farewell's point on the horizon
I want you in the exact wave that hides under another
uncovers itself   and finds its own form

I go   eternal flight   soul oh soul
any sight of land is only an illusion
and my untiring gaze delays itself in the blue

[Translated with Maria de Lourdes Magalhães]

"the day is born . . ." [103]

the day is born

the water is born
and slowly the sands
grow without sound

the day is born
iris
    the whole sea

growing into white light

[Translated with Maria de Lourdes Magalhães]

"I come . . ." [104]

I come from a dream country

a truth so clear
yet frightening

[Translated with Maria de Lourdes Magalhães]

only the dream can take me to you
it exalts me   exposes me to the wonder
it returns me to the ignorance
of knowing all
only the dream
can dazzle me

O beloved
only the dream
the dream spreads itself
it grows and makes you converge
towards me
to the full
within me
well-tied
knots
weightless gloves
of a natural silk
envelop you

O Master of my self
spirit of time
essence of being

[Translated with Maria de Lourdes Magalhães]

O moon
crystal ball
all-light

the evidence gleams
over the bride-head

O luminous small marble
in the hand of the bride
O bride-eye
in the small marble
in the hand
the whole
moon

poised in amidst stars
O white night
leaning
against the blue of this picture
where night populates night
with the night
in full whiteness

O light inside the light
you bring the darkness in your veil
dragging   haze   fog   clouds

O all in white
aflame
you cross the tail of comets on fire

O nebulous
dark night of whiteness   kindled gravity
O enchantment of the pure essence
night-flower   illumination   O polychromous

hidden dawn
bringing colour to the eclipse

you curl up in satin   purple robes
you caress the darkness
naked night

you drag the whiteness
                              whole
                                    O moon

Bengal-Roses

I am the rose in the rose
rose in a ring of roses
I want you rose-world windrose
I desire no other
on every bough
it appears full-hearted
the rose-bough centred on the centre
of being
a rose

a rosebush grows from within you
a rose-ring of a thousand roses desires you
inside the round rose
overwhelming with fragrances
with rose-leaves and perfume and velvet and silk
all embracing
they embrace and let the rose grow
assured of being
in the rose-creeper
that grows roses
of being within a thousand roses
that give you the heart

fully desired

it's one
they're two or three
all in all one
to leaf to un-petal
it inhales breathes
rose wants you rose

rose
the day grows
when you'll become
a rosebush

Book of Sorrows 108

tell me my heart where do you take me
what routes are these your routes
what anguish stirs inside you what wind brings you
tell me my heart where can I finally repose tell me
my heart where do the elves reside and the
fauns and mermaids the bright colours of dusk the
mists the pixies the castles the hills
always in full bloom
tell me my heart what routes are these your routes
which are not
mine what do you search for what
uneasiness lulls you what impossible journey
bids you tell me my heart that the sea is
deep and vast and that I don't exist because you
exist and you take me where I do not want to be taken
tell me my heart why do you take me without
my being aware of it without the calendars of time so that
if I could I would not exist that if I could I would not
feel that if I could I would have no heart

would have no heart

An Island Sails in My Soul

> her body is clothed
> with whelks and seaweed
> and it leaves behind on the sand
> silver footprints
> > Glória de Sant'Anna

an island sails through my soul
the ancient spirit of a voyaging ship

Penelope adorned with *m'siro**
gazes upon the tallest minaret
on the horizon

and on the wharf in ruins
the moored harbour of dreams
she ponders and thinks

through her fingers slide

strings with glass beads
strings of silver
strings of gold

the careful jewellery of silence

her face turned orient-wise
the linen wrapped around her body
the long-awaited monsoon
the abrupt wind
sail through her body

for she holds her hands together

---

* A white paste that women on the Island of Mozambique put on their faces as a sign
of beauty.

and draws astrolabes
diadems   necklaces
roses of sand

for she holds her hands together
between her strings
rosaries of silver
corals of dreams
ornaments   necklaces
she grows her many arms
she dances the wise bells on her ankles

the wind-swept linen   her slender body
undulates with the sea of infinite blues
and she perfumes the air with multiple geographies

she discovered the bulwark within herself
the wharf

Penelope adorned with *m'siro*
her hair is resplendent with stars
whelks   fish   spotted seashells
and it suggests fine cordage
entwined with seaweed

her face a sextant
her hands sailing through the pendants of pearly beads
her hands setting loose these strange homely spices

adorned with *m'siro*
Penelope records
the sparkling jewellery the silk the *kabayas*[†] the linen
on the sand
and she weaves her strings   her hair   her breasts
inside the indigo-purple turban
of the waters of the Indian Ocean

the orient begins with her face adorned with *m'siro*,

[†] *Malay*, sarongs.

saffron, ebony and anil
undulating whelks sail to the rhythm of her loins
her hands weave
a boat on her breast

the strings of silver
the strings of gold
the strings of dreams

fishing net
in the heart of the moored
water

it's not for Ulysses she awaits
but for a strange destiny
that the water spirit
will take her higher still than the clouds
eastwards westwards
into the centuries-old heart of the island
and enchant her and those lingering moments

will make her enamoured of him

Köln Concert in the Indian Ocean [110]

the *Concert in Cologne** is cast over the bay
and reaches the very clouds
the constant beating of the water
replicates the rising of the piano
in unceasing turmoil
I forget the rustle of the casuarinas
I forget all sounds
there's only the crescendo that's astir
in the piano deep within the water

and all of a sudden there is so much rain over the sea
it rains this rain that's warm and good
water that dilutes in the see-through water

the blue lead of a line on the horizon
draws out the strange contemplation of the years over
the years rolling with the notes on the piano
as though they were on an extraordinary odyssey

an unending whirlpool that's so tranquil and gentle
rests over this window
through which the entire seascape
of the Indian Ocean is filtered
intertwined with the *Concert in Cologne*

here in the bay
with the two boats sailing in the far distance
and as they sail so sail my transitory days,
the breathing of time beats slowly inside the water
the clouds rest in a long blue couch that has been blanched
and from the sky itself
they acquire the light of an uncertain becoming

---

* The recording of a piano concert by the composer Keith Jarrett originally
performed in Cologne in 1975.

I don't know if I desire to speak
all sounds have a preciseness that is lacking in speech
and so I resign myself to listening
ever since I was born I have listened to
all these voices that stride in silence through
the throat of the world and I shudder in admiration
at the multiple roots of their many senses
the clouds in the meantime have become a darker blue
and slowly a breeze stirs
alongside the shores of forgetfulness
I awake to the night and searchingly I gaze before the true
face of silence in these musical notes that run along the piano of a concert
that never ends
in the face of an proud solfeggio
I am returned to my redundancy
and I fall asleep in the keel of the sea

from this sleepiness
that is being in-the-process-of-becoming and is adrift
from this sleepiness
that is memory that's gone astray and is cast into the nets that I have left
and leave and shall leave all along the coast of this sea that returns me to the
state of a being in perpetual motion

I lay my head between my knees
and the sea continues to filter
through the balcony
encroaches on the table and floods the house
with the transmarine midnight blues, emerald and tourmaline of the
musical notes of Keith Jarrett
which vibrate as they knock against those bulwarks of the clouds
and the night laden with the couches of gold of the moon deranged
by all the light that has gravitated towards it
overfed with oranges and ghostly fruit
she glides over the water
as if in the direction of the infinite
slow and lingering she crosses the horizon of
silence where the sea discovers, farther still,
the island of Madagascar

she travels naked in her dhow of light
and is almost white
Ophelia-of-India
the whisperings of a dream
reclining in the light of her own death
she makes the muezzins cry
in the pinnacles of the mosques more to the north
they say Hamlet's gone mad
and with him the entire coast of the castle
of this Indian Ocean bulwark
musical seashells are blown in the direction of the east
and the music of Keith Jarrett dives into the sea
the long grand piano and the musical notes are heard
as if played at a particularly slow rotation

why does it forget me, the heart of being? why am I inhabited by such strange forgetting? suddenly the wind throws open the door and once again the Indian Ocean breeze gushes through the hand of Keith Jarrett sweeping the chords
his piano has emerged from the water and hurtles over the undulating tableland of this horizon where I will not find my end and to which I have belonged—as much as the syllabification of an absent music—ever since I was born
in this place
in these unending waves of memory
who knows if one day this water will become more serene
almost to the point that one can't hear the rustle
it makes when the lashing of the waves
comes close to the heart
comes close to this desired place
from where one leaves as if from a wharf
always voyaging on a ghost ship
which time brings us back to again and again
impossible quest in allegro andante ma non tropo
Jarrett makes the sea sigh and once again the sea floats in the waves of the semibreves which had vibrated in near-ecstasy to an E major when the moon, having once again undressed herself of clouds and revealed her undivided profile, surrendered to the tail end of this night which is perhaps

the beginning of the next night and the many layers of other slow nights
that are to come again

here in the stillness that has no memory
pierced only by the *Concert in Cologne*
in a time that's listened to
close to the heart that the jazz concert has secured to the horizons which
you Keith Jarrett have made disappear in my midnight-blue Indian Ocean
sailing through me with its luminous boats with tall sails
in far-distant and lengthy sweeping chords

in the loose stuff of the moon

I Was Named after a Ship [111]

for Ungulani Khosa
my story:

Ana Mafalda, the name of one of the empire's ships crossing two oceans, is what gave me birth. That's the name they gave me when I was transplanted from one hemisphere to the other. I was born on the intersection of fluid frontiers; I invented a cradle between waves. It was a name that gave me birth, it was a boat, it was the parting of the tides at the end of the nineteen-fifties.

      in Kano, my oldest brother tells me, there were snake charmers playing the fife and the snakes were dancing. I don't recall. At the time it was all silence and a flight over the waters. Two huge round awestruck eyes danced within me. In a photo from those days I am wearing a piquet dress and my little curls are intertwined with the sepia-coloured gaps in the picture.

      My blood bears the trace of my Jewish and Phoenician origins: my green eyes my mother's ocean, they don't lie, and neither does my father's cut-out Semitic profile. As a young child they took me to the Orient of the Indian Ocean.

      And I was born a second time.

      And that was where, in the north, on the frontier with the most ancient kingdom of Monomotapa where ores were once mined, that was where my boat was anchored. On the shore of Zambezi River, the Revugué River, the Moatize River. Like the operatic boat in Werner Herzog's Fitzcarraldo.

On the coal mines whose furnaces are like a trans-Atlantic descent into the centre of the earth, through the quartz stones and through the mica leaves and through the great river that crossed the underground tunnels of Munchém, I sail from Matundo to Tete. The hippos sleep slowly on the waters. At every name-place someone waves at me and, gazing back, I see that it is I. I am already another boat. Ana Mafalda. A barge or a motor canoe that's always crossing the river and, Zambezi-like, in still motion, with the long and nostalgic departure whistles of end-of-century Triumphal Odes and with the unpredictable waterfalls of the most ancient shoreline of the world.

Notes

The Sailor's First Speech. The poetry of exile is one of nostalgia and despair, often refined into a universal feeling of loss, one that transcends the loss of a particular country at a specific time. In this poem a sailor mediates on the loss of his land and the way he has become surrounded by the infinite space of a sea so 'boundless' that it becomes his condition of being. The blue, the ocean, the horizon, becomes the indices to his exile.

Bengal-Roses. The term 'rosas da China' can be translated to mean 'roses from China' or 'Chinese roses', although in English we know them as 'Bengal-roses'. It is important to keep these associations in mind when we read what Ana Mafalda Leite has said about her book. The words are taken from a speech she gave in Maputo in 1997: "I completed my most recent book of poetry last year. It is called *Roses from China*. Can there be some sort of irony in this topographical provocation? Deconstruct, disentangle, not Lisbon, not Maputo, not Luanda. Indochina? Bengal? *Roses from China*. The east within. They come from far. Yet they are close. Right here . . . Here are my roses; they are not our local *micaias* [knob-thorns], but instead roses derived from myth and eternal. They can be yours too. If you are willing to have them."[112]

FILIMONE MEIGOS (1960 -)

- *Poema & Kalash in Love* (1995[1990])
- *Globatinol-(Antídoto)—Ou o Garimpeiro do Tempo?* (2002)

The poet has had a varied career as a journalist, a secondary school teacher, an officer and political commissar in the army, a film actor, and, more recently, as an academic at the Universidade Eduardo Mondlane in Maputo. It is easy to see how this wide range of influences and interests are reflected in the poetry of Meigos, which is, at once, cosmopolitan, experimental, playful and zestful.

In Caliban's Footsteps [113]

"Since you've taught me your language, my role's to throw it back at you with clenched teeth"

On pathologizing each of our encounters
in the mornings heavy with the night dew
we are inoculated against the voice of what we are
WAPSWA MUTCHINE!
How your behaviour blemishes you
whenever you stand close to me
with your overseas prattle
a kick up the backside the language and the linguistic community?
And truth is raised to other exponents, is made triple, as far as
we know it is sovereign with all thousand versions and I don't know
how many conceptions, idealized, autonomous, real or enlivened,
persistent or debugged
(and lacking in all semantic rigour)
Simply hidden away. I find them
and seek them out once more
because this is the truth: going about discovering lies
"WAPSWA MUTCHINE!"
That's also our language, Prospero.

Flashback

Winnie* blew off her lid.
After they'd become omni-absent (kids and dollar signs)
as heavy with insinuations as are the facts
the acts grew in enormity.
On the breast of time, behold the (un)deserved medal:
—the confirmed truth.
In the hall of grand acts
see (camera off) time's shattered shop-window.
What about you, Mandela?

---

* Winnie Mandela.

"Let us start again in this manner . . ." [115]

Let us start again in this manner: if we have the sea, then our nation also includes other nations and its vocation is to love. Each and everyone of us is the sum up of our own selves, as well as of those who came through the sea-highway: tradition and modernity, difference and sobriety: sediment, moss, seaweed, octopus, mollusc, sand, boat, sail, wind, current, torrent, rain, emerald and shark: the sea and the ups and downs, and from, we can infer, tides and traditions.

How
"Go to the root (*radix*), and you'll see that tradition means to pass/to transmit the message . . . a type of DNA but with a context. Meiosis, mitosis, amoeba that replicates itself into a better species, that is to say, integrated in space."

ARMANDO ARTUR (1962 -)

- *Espelho dos Dias* (1986)
- *O Hábito das Manhãs* (1989)
- *Estrangeiros de Nós Próprios* (1996)

The poet published his first collection at the height of the 'civil war', when the country was engulfed by the horror of the butchery and terrible destruction wrought by the armed bandits. But Artur's poetry does not speak directly of these evil times, and it is not even overtly political; it instead speaks of nature and of the elements as emblematic signs of hope and justice. His early poetry was much influenced by the work of Sophia de Mello Breyner Andresen , a poet who has always held that describing the 'just equilibrium' of all things is itself also a political act because it points to a justice that is possible in the political world. Armando Artur's more recent work, while never discarding the positive influence of Andresen, is more confident, and the poetic voice that emerges is uniquely his own, at the same time that it is grounded in a Mozambican reality. Armando Artur lives in Maputo.

Childhood 116

Always the selfsame desire
to return to the seashores
of childhood:
the grasp of the fingers on the sand,
the joy of the eyes on the foam . . .

but how to return to the obliterated
foot-paths?
and how to return to the fountains
set on fire?

(on the underside of this desire
I behold myself
looking out for a future
I never manage to live!)

Your Body of Land and Scent of Sea [117]

Your body of land and scent of sea
where my ship is set afloat
and opens its sails and paths of freedom

your body of land and scent of sea
where my prow lets out secrets
into the pale wake on the water

your body of land and scent of sea
where my flag of dreams
bursts forth from the deep

your body of land and scent of sea
where once again my ship
prepares for new and lengthy journeys

in search of a day that is just, clean, whole

(let it be!)

The Secrets [118]

Let them come from centuries afar and from the oceans,
from the farthest and the deepest,
let the secrets of the unceasing waves
come to us

(for our glory
rests on the white sands on the shore)

Beach in Costa-do-Sol 119

Here in this place
the morning comes to me
in its fullness,
both round and geometric,
salty like the fragrance
of the sandalwood.

It is a morning for remembering.
Imagining the delirious light
in the blue heart of the sea
is a marvel in itself.
And with it is the womb of life,
the murmuring of the wind
and the first herald
of the ripeness of love.

Here in this place
the morning arises in a form
that is pure,
its smooth wings
are like seagulls in September.

(And within it
is the colourful luminosity of memory
and the white heat of hope.)

Nevertheless

while death lasts
I'll continue to believe and be obedient,
dedicated and profane.
It is terrible to be like the sun,
to silence the night,
abandon the stone,
warm the ground
and carry out the beginnings
of the rite.

For You 121

On the flashlight of your birthday
I shall bring you garlands of sand.
And to light
the wax-light of your age
I will simply bring
a torch of fireflies.
Because, after all,
I still bring in me that child
with rocks in his pockets.

(What more can you expect, mother,
if in the foot-paths
the dogs still bark?)

Let Us Bow, Then 122

[Let us bow, then]
before our gods;
for they allow us
to live this day
without the need for subterfuge.
For example,
it was augured for today
that we would wake up in a spell,
we would speak of the shape of periwinkles
and of children contained
on the inside of empty seashells.

For Sophia de Mello Breyner [123]*

The whelks
came and went
they went and they came
like a pendulum of the lost time.

What mystery was out there, after all?

(Would it really be the abetted
shipwreck of an impossible crime?)

—Perhaps. For the funereal march of the gods
resounds from the bell jar of the stars.

---

* Sophia de Mello Breyner Andresen, the distinguished Portuguese poet (1919 -
2004), noted for her lucid and rigorous handling of poetic language; a left-wing
Catholic, she was elected as a Socialist deputy to the Portuguese Constituent
Assembly soon after the April '74 Revolution.

EDUARDO WHITE (1963 -)

- *Amar sobre o Índico* (1984)
- *Homoíne* (1987)
- *O País de Mim* (1989)
- *Poemas da Ciência de Voar e da Engenharia de Ser Ave* (1992)
- *Os Materiais de Amor Seguido de Desafio à Tristeza* (1996)
- *Janela Para Oriente* (1999)
- *Dormir Com Deus e Um Navio na Língua* (2001)
- *O Homem a Sombra e a Flor & Algumas Cartas do Interior* (2004)
- *O Manual das Mãos* (2004)
- *Dos Limões Amarelos do Falo às Laranjas Vermelhas da Vulva* (2008)
- *A Fuga e a Húmida Escrita do Amor* (2009)

When the poet, then aged 21, published his first book, *Amar sobre o Índico* [Loving over the Indian Ocean], not only did the context of civil war and armed banditry make this sort of theme supposedly inappropriate, the poetry seemed to be the very negation of 'engaged' or 'committed' poetry that had dominated Mozambican letters in the period following independence. Eduardo White belongs in the tradition of poets like Glória de Sant'Anna, poets who do not deal with overt political themes—although it is true that Eduardo White did compose a long poem on the massacre at Homoíne. His subsequent books have refined this 'inward' voice and have developed his own individual way of making poetry. Eduardo White lives in Maputo.

"Happy are those . . ." [124]
—1984

Happy are those
who sing of love.

For theirs is the yearning for the unknown
and the unsure outline of the oceans.

extracts from **Homoíne** [125*]

      I
Our dead are many,
they are many inside
the common graves

and all of a sudden
the land is bleeding,
it thirsts and bleeds slowly

and it has live swords that whistle like the wind
and high walls that stanch the flow of time's each minute

our dead are many,
they are many inside
the common graves

and there's a huge bird that's become bewitched,
it's the slow bird of forgetfulness,
blood-bird, bird that rises above
the worms eating the insides of our dead

      II
Our dead are many,
ay, come and look,
they are many inside
the common graves

and the sadness rests on the coldness of the stones,
and there are screams scattered by many strange fears
and vultures fly in between the thick clouds
and bloodied ballerinas with knives at their fingertips

---

* Site of a massacre (on the 19th of July 1987) of innocent civilians by the South African-backed armed bandits.

and there's a naked child, a survivor,
it's the only child that lives and it has no relatives,
and it drinks,
and it sucks
at the tender breasts of the corpses,
at the hard genitals of the deceased,
the thick and yellowed milk,
the fatty and rotten milk
that quenches the thirst

      V
Oh, our dead are many,
they can't even be seen,
they are many inside
the common graves,

and there are cities of blood, cities without light,
and there are green flies filled with pus
that swell up and buzz,
that buzz and swell up,
swelling up and buzzing on the naked bodies

Ay, our dead are lonesome inside their husks,
they are lonesome and pure
they are cold and hard
and they're calling out to the living
and they're crying out to the just

with their sad hymns
with their mute hymns

"Mother, you gave me poetry for all eternity . . ."[126]

Mother, you gave me poetry for all eternity
even though it pains me to create it,
the magical beauty of words
—when I am worthy of them—
is why I live to sing today.

I am unable
to write grand epics of praise to life,
even though I am aware of how precious it is to live,
I say it here and now so it can be understood that the ground
where I stand upon, my land, brings terrible dreams and too much blood
being spilt and far too much ambition and if I write with some gentleness it
is because as I pronounce the words I dread already murdering them and I
need them alive and shining with fascination. Flying is not to permit the
music, the beauty, the word, to die and it is also an act of making up for the
writing of all this. Nothing can be more dazzling than this relation with life
and it is for this reason that I insist on the birds and try to be like them. I
like the way they dishevel my dismay, my despair, in the face of such
rottenness and also how they startle me when I prefer not to admit certain
things. I am happy, mother, you gave me poetry for all eternity even though
it pains me to write it here in this weary nation.

{25} With my back turned to the landscape outside, to the left of the door of the room where I write, opposite the window and the desk, a small bookcase imposes itself on me, as if by design. {26} Filled with grave-looking books, ready to be handled. The light which filters in draws a shadow over them. Arching and distorted. Books heaped on books, they remind me of the building I live in. The tenants, the characters in them. I should surely treat them with greater nobility. Like the old tome of *Os Lusíadas* [*The Lusiads*], from the year 1862, by my Olympian swimmer who with a front-crawl saved the lines[*] he had written and which I eventually would grow to love.

What need has a poet for glory when he can't write? Why does he need the sea when he can't see it?

[. . .] I savour the alcohol and I examine the light that runs through it. I feel like saying to it: Go and inspect {27} the interior of my darkness, go to that place of breath, of belly-ache and clay, go to the hull of tension. Diligent glass whose static clarity I envy. Alcohol helps me to police the sadness in embryo; it does not permit it to function. Alcohol prepares the insomnia for death, takes control of the gears, and delays the oncoming of sleepiness. Within me. For I have no defining ambition except for the magic of travel. To sleep on the banks of the Zambezi or urinate over the Nile.

To get to know Holland, liquid and in equilibrium, West Africa, and the streets of Zanzibar. And Japan. It is true: how I would like to see Japan other than through my window. Japan which is lilac. Which is another way of saying rain, lightsome, tremulous, iron, cement, snow or remoteness. It is right here: in a rice-yellow wooden bowl with stories engraved inside it. [. . .]

{32} In the continuation of seas your name, Japan, stands upright in the line I see before me; Japan which I do not know, oblique serpent: I shall stand

---

[*] The allusion is to the way Luis de Camões, after a shipwreck, is supposed to have swum ashore holding his only copy of *Os Lusíadas*.

closer to the window, bring my hands closer to that which does not remain of me in that place.

I want nothing else other than this mystery where I invent myself. I am feeling all right here, secure in this perennial place of my nostalgia. I have never been as far away as I in fact am; distance has never been as great as when I begin thinking inside this cold room. That is why it is dear to me and all the freedom it gives me. I like the darkness that lives within it, its tranquil, tarnished and lovely colour which I myself take on. I like the way it is a harbour for this ship of the imagination, its infinite window, as infinite as the sky that comes to me through it. I could sail past Durban from here, {33} round the Cape of Good Hope in a westward direction, bring back routes more ancient than those written down in my language. But there are so many things I do not want, so many strange things that mean nothing to me. [. . .]

{34} My Orient of so many different unities, mother of all creative energy, pantheon of the gods, how I can see it all from here: India, for example, beautiful and mysterious, sometimes Hellenic, sometimes Persian and European. Vishnu's India, as hot as the sun, as strong and tall as Shiva, but also indulgent and tender and generous like Krishna; India of syntheses, of colours which only she can distinguish and which she loves, of children and sages, of the *Chandala*[†] who grow into skeletons in amidst the misery and the sophistication; my syncretistic India {35} whom I now address and of whom I think in Sanskrit, her ruins of ballast, the bricks from her kilns, the cotton of the *khaddars*,[‡] I who wanted an indigo plantation, sunny and permanent on this sheet of paper like a swan,[§] a woman within me who would dance the traces of you, a musical scale in Khusrau's[**] sitar. In blue I dream of you as both *sanatana*[††] and erudite in the streets, in the markets selling paprika, ginger, cumin, in the human and mortal divinity of your

---

[†] The 'untouchables'.

[‡] Indian homespun cotton cloth.

[§] It is often thought that Indian ink is made from indigo. There used to be a Portuguese brand of Indian ink (a carbon ink, really) called 'Cisne' (Swan): this might explain the enigmatic image of the swan and the way it is associated with Indian ink.

[**] Amir Khusrau Dehlavi (1253-1325 AD), a classical Indian poet; it is often thought that Khusrau was the inventor of the sitar.

[††] 'Eternal'; Hinduism is known as the *sanatana dharma* (eternal faith).

fakirs, your snake-charmers. I dream of the sacred knowledge of my *ishta-devata*;[‡‡] I dream of the offerings of flowers and incense which I venerate you in [the temple of] Dasavatara or in Gupta; or I dream in your whole intangible essence. [. . .]

{39} Children by the safety stairs outside the flat are making deafening sounds; they are free from all this servitude I now feel, from ethical claims and a sense of the reality of destiny they'll have when they grow up. The cigarette disperses this weight in my head, summons a comfort that's imperfect but extensive, alien yet human. To live is not merely to feel the possibility of all that is unknown, all emotions and thoughts. Like this Orient towards which I aspire without really knowing why. This drowsy Orient, ignored, patient and lost within me. Yes, this ancestral Orient which I seek out in the same way that I seek out my own ancestry. Vague, yet so well examined, so real: in what I have lived and remember, or I want to revisit, or, instead, what I want to become impossibly true and present. Nothing can return. I know it. Nothing can be reborn {40} in the same manner that something was born. Nothing can have, anew, the horror of the end. [. . .]

{62} [. . .] I leave Saigon in a junk, with supplies of rice cakes, fried banana and some salted fish. I leave Saigon and my mulatto with some sadness; clap-ridden, he was crying into a Red Cross poster: I'm going to Boston minus a leg, stoned with life itself, I lost my life killing in the name of the old white man in a funeral suit and top hat and reading, and from reading Ginsberg, fucked because they'd taken everything away from him and had never received anything in return. Venereal Saigon of napalm in Lennon's song, putting bombs in the home of the English royal family and saying he was better than Jesus and masturbating with his sunglasses with Japan through Yoko, my Saigon undefeated even by Marilyn Monroe's papaws, chafed from sleeping with the whole of America or from smelling America through a white tube, alone redeeming herself from Martin Luther King's old black blood. Saigon of shame, terrorist Saigon {63} of malaria, showing off against the pinkie-sized mosquito-ish Communist Ho Chin Min, invisible Saigon, Machiavellian, which is not to say that Machiavelli was to blame for this. Maoist until it suits her, Saigon of the bananas peeling off the world and vomiting it out in Broadway, tap-dancing with the resigned Fred Astaire, in the adolescent blondes of New York greasily hysterical with

---

[‡‡] Personal deity.

Frank Sinatra's golden johnny or in the voluminous manioc of Jimi Hendrix's teeth playing the "The Star-Spangled Banner". Sad and sick Saigon, but unbowed in Phnom Penh and in the torn boots of the citizen Giap, who was oriental in everything and mystical and strong. I can see you from here and you don't know it; with a ship ready to sail from the centre of the breast and the suitcases of conscience which still need to be unpacked.

References

[1] Lesego Rampolokeng, *End Beginnings* [tape recording] (Yeoville, Johannesburg: Shifty Records, 1992), side 2.

[2] cited by Nelson Saúte, "O Escritor Moçambicano e a Língua Portuguesa," *Tempo*, 11 Fevereiro 1991, p. 43; my translation.

[3] Sophia de Mello Breyner Andresen, *Obra Poética I* (Lisboa: Caminho, 1991), pp. 7-8; my translation.

[4] [José Pedro da Silva] Campos Oliveira, "O Pescador de Moçambique," in *O Mancebo e Trovador Campos Oliveira*, ed. by Manuel Ferreira (Lisboa: Imprensa Nacional-Casa da Moeda, 1985), pp. 111-2.

[5] Rui de Noronha, "Surge et Ambula," *África*, 8 Fevereiro 1936, p. 12.

[6] Reinaldo Ferreira, "Roma 475," *Poemas* (Lisboa: Portugália, 1962), p. 149.

[7] Ferreira, "Se eu nunca disse que os teus dentes. . .," *Poemas*, p. 13.

[8] Ferreira, "Quando as fachadas, tumulares de pardas. . .," *Poemas*, p. 39.

[9] Ferreira, "Café do cais . . .," *Poemas*, p. 37.

[10] Ferreira, "Copélia," *Poemas*, p. 17.

[11] José Craveirinha, "Esperança," *Karingana ua Karingana* (Lisboa/Maputo: Edições 70/INLD, 1982), p. 31.

[12] Craveirinha, "Os Poros da Peste," *Karingana*, p. 34.

[13] Craveirinha, "Fábula," *Karingana*, p. 18.

[14] Craveirinha, "Civilização," *Karingana*, p. 24.

[15] Craveirinha, "Oh! Carmen de Diego," original typescript, 1992.

[16] José Craveirinha, "Quando o José Pensa na América," original typescript, 1992.

[17] Craveirinha, "Maria Sende," *Karingana*, p. 62.

[18] Craveirinha, "Grito Negro," *Xigubo* (Maputo: INLD, 1980), pp. 13-14.

[19] Craveirinha, "Imprecação," *Xigubo*, p. 24.

[20] Craveirinha, "Poema do Futuro Cidadão," *Xigubo*, p. 18.

[21] Craveirinha, "Cantiga do Batelão," *Xigubo*, p. 36.

[22] Craveirinha, "Cântico do Pássaro Azul de Sharpeville," *Karingana*, pp. 78-9.

[23] Craveirinha, "Elegia à Minha Avó Fanisse," *Xigubo*, pp. 45-6.

[24] Craveirinha, "Mamana Saquina," *Karingana*, pp. 89-90.

[25] Craveirinha, "Quero Ser Tambor," *Karingana*, pp. 123-4.

[26] José Craveirinha, "Martin Luther King," original typescript, 1992.

[27] José Craveirinha, "Cela 1," *Cela 1* (Lisboa: Edições 70, 1980), p. 56.

[28] Craveirinha, "Metamorfose," *Cela*, p. 55.

[29] Craveirinha, "Lustro," *Cela*, p. 49.

[30] José Craveirinha, "Nossa Cidade," *Caliban* 3/4 (1972): p. 113.

[31] José Craveirinha, "Excerto de Álbum de Autógrafos para um Menino Vietnamita," original typescript, 1992.

[32] José Craveirinha, "As Saborosas Tanjarinas d' Inhambane," in *Antologia da Nova Poesia Moçambicana*, ed. by Fátima Mendonça and Nelson Saúte (Maputo: Associação dos Escritores Moçambicanos, 1994), pp. 215-6.

[33] Craveirinha, "Terra de Canaã," *Antologia*, pp. 211-2.

[34] José Craveirinha, "Colares de Pneus," original typescript, 1992.

[35] José Craveirinha, "Why?," original typescript, 1992.

[36] Craveirinha, "Comunicado de Cuíto Cuanavale," *Antologia*, pp. 228-8.

[37] Craveirinha, "Memento," *Antologia*, pp. 225-5.

[38] José Craveirinha, "Hienas e Lanhos," *Maria* (Lisboa: Caminho, 1998), p. 112.

[39] José Craveirinha, "De Profundis," *Maria*, p. 53.

[40] José Craveirinha, "De Profundis," *Babalaze das Hienas* (Maputo: Associação dos Escritores Moçambicanos, 1997), p. 24.

[41] Craveirinha, "Aldeia Queimada," *Babalaze das Hienas*, p. 32.

[42] Craveirinha, "Gula," *Babalaze*, p. 22.

[43] Craveirinha, "Barbearia," *Babalaze*, p. 45.

[44] Craveirinha, "Eles Foram Lá," *Babalaze*, p. 19.

[45] Glória de Sant'Anna, "Vitral," *Amaranto: Poesia 1951-1983* (Lisboa: Imprensa Nacional-Casa da Moeda, 1988), p. 39

[46] de Sant'Anna, "Desenho na Areia," *Amaranto*, p. 74.

[47] de Sant'Anna, "Condição," *Amaranto*, p. 63.

[48] de Sant'Anna, "Marinha," *Amaranto*, p. 61.

[49] de Sant'Anna, "Poema Agreste," *Amaranto*, p. 111.

[50] de Sant'Anna, "Nocturno," *Amaranto*, p. 134.

[51] de Sant'Anna, "Poema Oitavo," *Amaranto*, p. 171.

[52] de Sant'Anna, "Poema Sexto," *Amaranto*, pp. 167-8.

[53] de Sant'Anna, "Desde que o Mundo," *Amaranto*, p. 185.

[54] de Sant'Anna, "Poema do Mar," *Amaranto*, p. 190.

[55] de Sant'Anna, "Mar," *Amaranto*, p. 202.

[56] de Sant'Anna, "Segundo Poema da Solidão," *Amaranto*, p. 200.

[57] de Sant'Anna, "mas por outro lado poderia romper-se também. . .," *Amaranto*, p. 235.

[58] de Sant'Anna, "em cnossos havia um homem. . .," *Amaranto*, p. 278.

[59] de Sant'Anna, "no azul puro do mar. . . ," *Amaranto*, p. 266.

[60] Glória de Sant'Anna, "Moenda," original typescript, 1997.

[61] Glória de Sant'Anna, "O Moinho do Castelo," original typescript, 1997.

[62] Glória de Sant'Anna, "O Pescador Velho," in *Primeiro Livro de Poesia*, ed. by Sophia de Mello Breyner Andresen (Lisboa: Caminho, 1993), p. 136.

[63] Glória de Sant'Anna, "Poema," original typescript, 1993.

[64] Glória de Sant'Anna, "Erótica," *Algures no Tempo* (Óvar: n.p, 2005), pp. 31-2.

[65] de Sant'Anna, "Musicando Arrabil," *Algures no Tempo*, p. 27.

[66] Noémia de Sousa, "Patrão," *Sangue Negro* (roneoed notebook), unpaginated.

[67] de Sousa, "Samba," *Sangue.*

[68] Noémia de Sousa, "Poema para Rui de Noronha," in *50 Poetas Africanos,* ed. by Manuel Ferreira (Lisboa: Plátano Editora, 1989), 352-4.

[69] Noémia de Sousa, "Poema da Infância Distante," *Tempo,* 30 Setembro 1990, pp. 46-7.

[70] de Sousa, "Magaíça," *50 Poetas,* pp. 354-5.

[71] Noémia de Sousa, "A Mulher que Ri à Vida e à Morte," in *A Meu Ver,* ed. by Carlos Pinto Coelho (Lisboa: Pégaso Editores, 1992), p. 50.

[72] Rui Knopfli, "Velho Poema da Cidade do Ouro," *O País dos Outros* (Lourenço Marques: private edition, 1959), pp. 13-4.

[73] Knopfli, "Epigrama," *País,* p. 18.

[74] Rui Knopfli, "Mangas Verdes com Sal," *Memória Consentida* (Lisboa: Imprensa Nacional-Casa da Moeda, 1982), p. 275.

[75] Knopfli, "O Cão da Angústia," *Memória,* p. 247.

[76] Knopfli, "Progresso," *Memória,* p. 264.

[77] Knopfli, "Canção de Ariel," *Memória,* p. 347.

[78] Knopfli, "Mesquita Grande," *Memória,* p. 341.

[79] Knopfli, "Terraço da Misericórdia," *Memória,* p. 339.

[80] Knopfli, "Pátria," *Memória,* pp. 363-4.

[81] Rui Knopfli, "Cambaco," *O Monhé das Cobras* (Lisboa: Caminho, 1997), p. 28.

[82] Knopfli, "O Monhé das Cobras,"*Monhé,* p. 23.

[83] Rui Knopfli, "O Nobel e Nós," *Jornal de Letras,* 11 Fevereiro 1992, p. 31.

[84] Rui Nogar, "O Jacaré," in *Antologia da Nova Poesia Moçambicana,* ed. by Fátima Mendonça and Nelson Saúte (Maputo: Associação dos Escritores Moçambicanos, 1994), pp. 369-71.

[85] Nogar, "Tempo," *Antologia,* pp. 375-6.

[86] Heliodoro Baptista, "A Aldeia," *Por Cima de Toda a Folha* (Maputo: Associação dos Escritores Moçambicanos, 1987), pp. 13-5.

[87] Baptista, "As Outras Mãos," *Por Cima,* pp. 55-6.

[88] Baptista, "Maiakowski," *Por Cima,* p. 57.

[89] Heliodoro Baptista, "A uma Ingénua Nórdica," *A Filha de Thandi* (Maputo: Associação dos Escritores Moçambicanos, 1991),pp. 71-2.

[90] Maria Manuela de Sousa Lobo, "Magaíça-Kid," in *No Reino de Caliban III,* ed. by Manuel Ferreira (Lisboa: Plátano Editora, 1985), pp. 458-9.

[91] Lobo, "Dois Anti-Sonetos de Cobras e Lagartos," *Reino,* pp. 457-8.

[92] Luís Carlos Patraquim, "Metamorfose," *Monção* (Maputo: INLD, 1980), pp. 27-8.

[93] Patraquim, "afasto as cortinas da tarde. . .," *Monção,* p. 38.

[94] Luís Carlos Patraquim, "penso as tuas mãos como guelras no mar. . .," *A Inadiável Viagem* (Maputo: Associação dos Escritores Moçambicanos, 1985), p. 16

[95] Patraquim, "Canção," *Viagem*, pp. 21-2.

[96] Patraquim, "Ode Indica," *Viagem*, p. 63.

[97] Luís Carlos Patraquim, "Elegia Carnívora," *Vinte e Tal Novas Formulações e uma Elegia Carnívora* (Lisboa: Juntamon, 1991), pp. 50-2.

[98] Patraquim, "Ilha, corpo, mulher...," *Vinte*, p. 41.

[99] Patraquim, "Foste uma vez...," *Vinte*, p. 42.

[100] Luís Carlos Patraquim, "Des-soneto," *Lidemburgo Blues* (Lisboa: Caminho, 1997), p. 41.

[101] Luís Carlos Patraquim, "Lidemburgo Blues," *Lidemburgo*, p. 13.

[102] Ana Mafalda Leite, "Primeira Fala do Marinheiro," *Canções de Alba* (Lisboa: Vega, 1989), 29.

[103] Leite, "nasce o dia...," *Canções*, p. 23.

[104] Ana Mafalda Leite, "venho...," *Também com Noivas*, in Roberto Chichorro, Ana Mafalda Leite, and Luís Carlos Patraquim, *Mariscando Luas* (Lisboa: Vega, 1992), p. 65.

[105] Leite, "apenas o sonho...," *Mariscando*, p. 113.

[106] Leite, "ó lua...," *Mariscando*, pp. 75-6.

[107] Ana Mafalda Leite, "Rosas da China," *Rosas da China* (Lisboa: Quetzal Editores, 1999), pp. 17-8.

[108] Leite, "Livro de Mágoas," *Rosas*, p. 68.

[109] Ana Mafalda Leite, "Navega-me a Alma uma Ilha," *Passaporte do Coração* (Lisboa: Quetzal Editores, 2002), pp. 37-40.

[110] Leite, "*Koln Concert* no Indíco," *Passaporte*, pp. 113-6.

[111] Ana Mafalda Leite, "Tenho o Nome de um Barco," *Livro de Encantações* (Lisboa: Caminho, 2005), pp. 36-7.

[112] Ana Mafalda Leite, "A Minha Herança Moçambicana," Speech given at the Universidade Eduardo Mondlane, Maputo, 30 Maio 1997.

[113] Filimone Meigos, "Na Senda de Caliban," *Poema & Kalash in Love* (Maputo: Associação dos Escritores Moçambicanos, 1995), p. 28.

[114] Meigos, "Flash Back," *Poema*, p. 80.

[115] Filimone Meigos, "Recomecemos assim...," *Globatinol-(Antídoto)—Ou o Garimpeiro do Tempo?* (Maputo: Imprensa Universitária UEM, 2002), 25.

[116] Armando Artur, "Infância," *Espelho dos Dias* (Maputo: Associação dos Escritores Moçambicanos, 1986), p. 23.

[117] Armando Artur, "O Teu Corpo de Terra e Maresia," *O Hábito das Manhãs* (Maputo: Associação dos Escritores Moçambicanos, 1990), p. 32.

[118] Artur, "Os Segredos," *Hábito*, p. 13.

[119] Artur, "Praia da Costa-do-Sol," *Hábito*, p. 11.

[120] Armando Artur, "Contudo," *Estrangeiros de Nós Próprios* (Maputo: Associação dos Escritores Moçambicanos, 1996), p. 28.

[121] Artur, "Para Ti," *Estrangeiros*, p. 43.

[122] Artur, "Acocoremo-nos Então," *Estrangeiros*, p. 22.

[123] Artur, "Para Sophia de Mello Breyner," *Estrangeiros*, p. 42.

[124] Eduardo White, "Felizes os homens . . .," in *Antologia da Nova Poesia Moçambicana*, ed. by Fátima Mendonça and Nelson Saúte (Maputo: Associação dos Escritores Moçambicanos, 1994), p. 88.
[125] Eduardo White, *Homoíne* (Maputo: Associação dos Escritores Moçambicanos, 1987), unpaginated.
[126] Eduardo White, "Mãe que me deste a poesia por eternidade. . .," *Poemas da Ciência de Voar e da Engenharia de Ser Ave* (Lisboa: Caminho, 1992), p. 29,
[127] Eduardo White, *Janela para Oriente* (Lisboa: Caminho, 1999), pp. 25-27, 32-35, 39-40, 62-63.

Credits

Acknowledgement is made to the following poets who have given their written permission for translations from their work to appear in this anthology: Armando Artur; the late José Craveirinha; the late Rui Knopfli; Ana Mafalda Leite; Filimone Meigos, Luís Carlos Patraquim; Elsa de Noronha (for Rui de Noronha); Glória de Sant'Anna; the late Noémia de Sousa; Maria Manuela de Sousa Lobo; and Eduardo White. Every effort was made to locate the heirs of Reinaldo Ferreira and Rui Nogar, but I would still be interested to hear from them. Heliodoro Baptista never responded to my letter, which I interpreted as a tacit acceptance. The painter Roberto Chichorro has also given permission for one his paintings to appear on the cover of the anthology.